A Christian Critic Book
$1.25

JOSEPH HOUPPERT

JOHN HENRY

NEWMAN

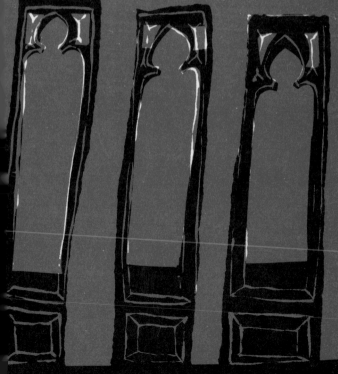

john henry newman

john henry newman

Edited by
JOSEPH W. HOUPPERT

Contributors

NORTHROP FRYE
WALTER J. ONG, S.J.
HAROLD M. PETITPAS
FRANK O'MALLEY
JOHN PICK

BX
4705
.N5
H66

B. HERDER BOOK CO.
314 NORTH JEFFERSON
ST. LOUIS, MISSOURI 63103

The Christian Critic Series is under the general editorship of Harry J. Cargas, Director of the Foreign Student Program, Saint Louis University

Contents

INTRODUCTION

A leader during his lifetime, a legend after his death, John Henry Newman typifies the man of integrity and commitment. Poet and preacher, historian and novelist, educator and apologist, Newman himself best expressed the nature of his dedication: "God has created me to do Him some definite service; He has committed some work to me which He has not committed to another. I have my mission—I may never know it in this life, but I shall be told in the next." As a spokesman for religious and humanistic values in an age of scientific rationalism, Newman did more than merely reiterate the eternal verities. On the occasions when he did so, however, he charged them with a rhetorical eloquence seldom equaled in our century. But is not for his grand style that Newman is remembered today; it is, rather, for his original contributions to educational theory, church history, literature and humanity.

Born in London in 1801, Newman received his early education at Ealing before entering Trinity College, Oxford, in 1816. Poor health caused him to do poorly on his examinations in 1820; therefore, instead of pursuing the law as his father had hoped, Newman decided to enter the church. Following his ministerial training at Oriel College, Newman was made curate of St. Clement's Church in 1824; but in 1826 he relinquished his curacy to return to Oriel as a Tutor. Here Newman became friends with the two men who exerted the most influence on his early religious attitudes—Hurrell Froude and John Keble. Under their direction Newman began to turn away

from rationalism and seek truth in Christian tradition an
the Church Fathers.

Newman's interest in the Church Fathers resulted, i
1833, in the *Arians of the Fourth Century,* a work i
which he noted significant similarities between the Aria
heresy of the fourth century and the growing liberalis
of his own nineteenth century. In the same year appeare
a series of *Tracts for the Times* which, although pub
lished anonymously, were written by Newman, Froud
Keble, Pusey, and others of their persuasion. An er
croaching government was threatening the structure of th
Anglican establishment and the *Tracts* were written t
demonstrate that the Anglican Bishops were the legitimat
successors of the apostles and thus deserved the suppo
of the people. But the defense of the Anglican episcopac
which Newman entered upon was ultimately to lead hir
in another direction. As he read further in the Churc
Fathers he began to doubt the validity of the Anglica
Church. Finally, in 1845, Newman converted to Roma
Catholicism.

Newman joined the Oratorians, a monastic order whic
fostered writing and study, and in 1851 was asked to es
tablish a Catholic University in Dublin. Although th
project ultimately failed, Newman left, in his *Idea of*
University, a substantial body of writing on the subjec
of education. For the next decade Newman wrote littl
of lasting value, but in 1863 the English novelist Charle
Kingsley published a blistering attack on Newman an
the Roman clergy. Newman's reply, the *Apologia pro Vit*
Sua, takes its place with Augustine's *Confessions* as on
of the world's most eloquent spiritual autobiographies
Newman's last major work, *A Grammar of Assent,* ap
peared in 1870. Like most of his other writings, this, too
bears testimony to Newman's life-long struggle against th
forces of rationalism, liberalism and materialism.

Although Newman's true mission may never have bee
revealed to him in this life, the world, at least, acknowl

dged his worth. In 1877 Trinity College made him a Fellow, and in 1879 Pope Leo XIII elevated him to the rank of Cardinal. His last years spent in relative obscurity, John Henry Newman died on August 11, 1890.

The essays in this collection were chosen for their inherent excellence and comprehensiveness. Although Newman's writings fill some forty volumes, the essays here presented touch on most of the important moments in Newman's rich and varied career.

Northrop Frye's essay on spiritual authority sets the stage for Father Walter J. Ong's analysis of the intellectual background of Newman's *Essay on the Development of Christian Doctrine*. Concerned as it is with the nature of ecclesiastical authority in the nineteenth century, Professor Frye's essay is broad in scope and provides the reader with a perspective against which Newman may be measured in light of his predecessors and contemporaries.

Father Ong's essay on the intellectual background of Newman's *Essay on the Development of Christian Doctrine*, though focusing on one work, can hardly be called narrow. In his usual fashion, Father Ong ranges far and wide, bringing to his subject a breath of vision and clarity of expression. Published in the same year that Newman became a Roman Catholic, the *Essay on Development* is crucial in his canon, and Father Ong helps us to see it more clearly.

As a novelist, Newman's powers were, indeed, modest. Few, if any, readers can be found for *Loss and Gain* or *Callista*. But as a poet, Newman displayed considerable talent. "Lead, Kindly Light" and "The Dream of Gerontius" have lost little of their original appeal. Two essays in this collection are devoted to Newman's literary theories and practice: Harold Petitpas's "Newman's Idea of Literature" and John Pick's "Newman the Poet."

Professor Petitpas examines Newman's critical theories in light of a humanist's spectrum, and explains why Newman argued so strongly for the inclusion of literary studies

3

in a university education. In an age captivated by th "new criticism" and so influenced by science that com putors are being trained as literary critics, Newman's em phasis on the humanizing role of literature bears fresh consideration.

Professor Pick examines Newman's poems in order t explain why the poetic powers that could produce "The Dream of Gerontius" could also produce such inferio poems as "St. Paul at Melita." By investigating the milie which gave rise to Newman the poet, Professor Pick de liniates the forces which molded the poetry, both goo and bad.

Finally, Frank O'Malley's "The Thinker in the Church The Spirit of Newman" gathers up many of the idea discussed in the preceding essays and re-examines them i light of the rapidly changing religious world of the twen tieth century. Professor O'Malley focuses upon Newman' meaning for contemporary man and points out how much there is of value if we but take the time to look.

I would like to express my gratitude to the Genera Research Board of the University of Maryland whose as sistance has made this work possible.

Joseph W. Houppert
University of Maryland

4

Northrop Frye

THE PROBLEM OF SPIRITUAL AUTHORITY

IN THE NINETEENTH CENTURY

The source of actual or "temporal" authority in society is seldom hard to locate. It is always in the near vicinity of whatever one pays one's taxes to. As long as it can be believed that might is right, and that the tax-collecting power is not to be questioned, there is no separate problem of spiritual authority. But the thesis that might is right, even when as carefully rationalized as it is in Hobbes, has seldom been regarded as much more than an irresponsible paradox. There has almost certainly never been a period in history when the taxpayer did not try to cheat the publican, and even the desire to cheat raises the question of what kinds of authority may be thought of as overriding the actual one. For self-interest also has a separate authority.

Spiritual authority is usually connected, of course, with religion, God being normally thought of as a sovereign spirit. Our cultural tradition has inherited from the Old Testament a conception of the will of God which may

This study, abridged slightly here, is reprinted with permission of the copyright owners, the University of Chicago Press, from *Literary Views: Critical and Historical Essays,* ed. by Carroll Camden (Published for William Marsh Rice University by the University of Chicago Press, Chicago, 1964), pp. 145-58.

often be in the sharpest possible opposition to the will of man, especially an Egyptian or Babylonian or Philistine will. But if a religion can find an accredited human representative, the two kinds of authority again tend to merge. The medieval theory of the pope's right to temporal power and the post-Renaissance conception of the divine right of kings are examples of an effort to make the spiritual order a guarantee of the stability of the temporal one. As far as the normal workings of the human mind can go, the will of God differs in degree but not in kind from the will of man, and the metaphors applied to it, such as the metaphor of divine "sovereignty," are drawn from the more primitive forms of human society. When Greek philosophers began to frame ethical conceptions of justice and righteousness, they ran into similar problems. Their traditional gods, as they appear in Homer, still had all the arbitrary and whimsical quality of a human aristocracy, and submitting to a human conqueror would not be psychologically very different from praying to Poseidon the irascible earth-shaker. In Christianity the human product of spiritual authority is supposed to be charity, but Christian charity has usually been, down to quite recent times, supported by temporal power, and it may be significant that the word "charity" itself has come to mean chiefly a form of voluntary taxation.

Ordinary social consciousness usually begins in a sense of antithesis between what the ego wants and what society will allow it to have. Hence temporal authority comes to the individual first of all in the form of an external compulsion. In this stage freedom is identified with the ego's side of this antithesis. But education, and more particularly education of the reason, introduces us to a form of necessity or compulsion which is not opposed to freedom but seems to be rather another aspect of it. To assent to the truth of a geometrical demonstration is psychologically a contrast to assenting to the will of a social superior. Hence reason can do what faith, hope, and even love by themselves cannot do: present us with the model or pattern of an authority which appeals to the mind but not to the body, which compels but does not enforce. Such authority confers dignity on the person who accepts it, and such dignity has no context of hierarchy, nobody at whose expense the dignity is achieved.

The nineteenth-century social and political writers in Great Britain had inherited from Milton a conception of spiritual authority of this sort, and a singularly lucid and powerful one. For Milton the source of spiritual authority was revelation from God, more particularly the revelation of the gospel which had spiritualized the law, and delivered those under the gospel from the sense of external constraint. St. Paul tells us that where the spirit of the Lord is, there is liberty, and those under the gospel should do as they like, because what they like to do is the will of God, not the illusory pseudo-acts suggested by passion or selfishness. For Milton, again, the accredited human agent of spiritual authority is the church in the sense of the society of individuals who are under the gospel, among whom the one who has authority is the apostle or saint, which according to Milton is what the New Testament means by an *episcope* or overseer. Such authority clearly has no relevance to magistrates or penal codes. Revelation from God accommodates itself to man primarily in the form of reason. Reason manifests itself in the decisive acts of a free life ("Reason is but choosing," Milton says in *Areopagitica,* annexing Aristotle's conception of *proairesis* of the Christian *logos*), and as revelation is the opposite of mystery, there is no conflict between spiritual authority and reason. A revelation from an infinite mind may transcend the reason of a finite one, but does not contradict or humiliate it.

Human society, as Milton saw it, is conditioned by the inertia of original sin to seek the habitual and customary, to do things because they have been done before, to make an idol of tradition. The impact of revelation, coming through reason, is always subversive and revolutionary: it is bound to shake up the somnambulism of habit and confront it with the eternal opposition of God and fallen man. Such reason is also liberty, which man does not naturally want, but which God wants him to have. Purely social changes are, at best, gradual adjustments: genuine liberty is sudden and apocalyptic: "In state many things at first are crude and hard to digest, which only time and deliberation can supple and concoct. But in religion, wherein is no immaturity, nothing out of season, it goes far otherwise. The door of grace turns upon smooth hinges, wide opening to send out, but soon shutting to recall the precious offers of mercy to a nation" (*The Reason of Church Government*). Temporal authority, however essential, is also provisional, the result of the permanent emergency in human affairs caused by the Fall. It can never be accepted as an end in itself: the reason why it is there is stated in scripture, and all non-scriptural ways of trying to justify it are suspect. There is no inherent authority, in other words, in tradition or custom or precedent, on which temporal authority may rest as a basis. Hence no church which bases its claim to authority on tradition can be a genuine embodiment of revelation. Milton's regicide pamphlet, *The Tenure of Kings and Magistrates,* is a work of extraordinary originality of thought, outlining an early theory of contract and being one of the earliest efforts to try to give some functional place to revolution in history. But even this involves an appeal to precedent, and Milton embarks on an appeal to precedent with the greatest unwillingness: "But because it is the vulgar folly of men to desert their own reason, and shutting their eyes, to think they see best with other men's, I shall show, by such examples as ought to have most weight with us, what has been done in this case heretofore."

We have, then, in Milton, a spiritual authority with its roots in revelation and manifesting itself largely in reason, and a temporal authority which is to be acknowledged

...nd obeyed in its own sphere, but should not be rationalized by arguments drawn from precedent or custom. Temporal authority is primarily something that is there, whether we like it or not. If we don't like it, we turn to a conception of spiritual authority and subordinate the temporal power to it as far as possible, if only in our own minds. If we do like it or want to defend it, on the other hand, we tend to see in tradition, custom, habit, in short the process by which temporal authority came to be, some kind of inherent right. We may note in passing that if social revolution is not, for Milton, organically related to precedents, it is not organically related to the future either. The rebellions of the Jews against their overlords, as recorded in the Old Testament, had varying degrees of success, but none were permanently successful. Hence the significance of such a rebellion is typological, manifesting the power of the true God for and at the moment. The extent to which Milton was able to reconcile himself with the failure of the revolution of his own day is perhaps indicated in *Samson Agonistes,* where the temporary victory of Samson in destroying the Philistine temple has this kind of significance.

In the eighteenth century the conception of the natural society in Bolingbroke and Rousseau brought a new kind of revolutionary dialectic into social argument. Rousseau thought of man in his context as a child of nature, and not, as Milton did, in his context as a child of God whose original state was civilized. It was reason and nature that were associated in his thought, not reason and revelation, and the original free and equal society of man was not something intended for man by God which man irrevocably lost, but something man still has the power to recapture. Rousseau's thought resembles Milton's only in associating reason and revolution, and in thinking of reason as essentially the vision in the light of which the free act is performed. It is with the counter-revolutionary thought that developed in Britain in opposition to Rous-

9

seau, particularly in Burke, that the problem of spiritual
authority in the nineteenth century begins.

For Burke, in almost direct contrast to Milton, the
first justification for temporal authority consists in the
fact that it is there: the right underlying its might, therefore, is the process of tradition and precedent that has
brought it into being. The social contract of any society
"is collected from the form into which the particular society has been cast." Any developed society is found to
consist of various classes, and the tendency of each class
is to promote its own interest by acting "merely by their
will." This creates tyranny, whether exerted by the king
(who is historically a class in himself), by the nobility,
or, as in France, by the "people," which means one class
or group of people. The source of spiritual authority for
Burke, therefore, is to be found, not so much in tradition as such, as in a kind of *telos*, a sense of belonging
to a social organism whose health is preserved by maintaining a balance of power among the different organs.
The health of the social structure is the end of all social
action from any class, and the standard by which such
action should be judged. Revolutionary action, which sets
free an automatic and unconditioned will, is to society
what the cancerous growth of tissue is in the individual.
A social organism of this kind is the only genuine form
of natural society, for nature is to be thought of as an
order that preserves constancy in change by a process of
continuous repair. "Thus, by preserving the method of
nature in the conduct of the state, in what we improve
we are never wholly new; in what we retain, we are never
wholly obsolete."

Two factors in Burke's thought are particularly relevant here. In Milton, the current of liberty, so to speak,
normally flows in a deductive direction, from revelation
to reason, and from reason to social action. For Burke,
liberty can only be preserved by the inductive, empirical

10

even *ad hoc* procedures of the political action that operates on the basis of what is there: prudence is the greatest of political virtues, and prejudice the only valuable form of deductive thinking. It is the revolutionary action leading to tyranny which is deductive, like the "metaphysical" French Revolution which had begun with a set of major premises about the abstract rights of man, and had then attempted "a decomposition of the whole civil and political mass, for the purpose of originating a new civil order out of the first elements of society." Hence reason, given its full deductive and speculative head, is not an emancipating but a destructive and ultimately enslaving power in politics. Spiritual authority, at least, is something to which we owe loyalty, and loyalty is not primarily rational; hence society is held together by profounder forces than the reason can express or reach.

In the second place, most temporal authority is vested in the ascendant class: this class is faced with a strong revolutionary bid for power coming from further down in society: the maintenance of the health of the social organism, which means the maintenance of spiritual authority, is therefore bound up with preserving the existing rights and privileges of the ascendant class. "We must suppose [society] to be in that state of habitual social discipline, in which the wiser, the more expert, and the more opulent conduct, and by conducting enlighten and protect the weaker, the less knowing, and the less provided with the goods of fortune." Burke goes on to say that "the state of civil society, which necessarily generates this aristocracy, is a state of nature"—that is, once again, the genuine form of natural society. The ascendant class includes the church, as for Burke the church is a continuous social institution, and its spiritual authority is inconceivable without that continuity. Hence Burke says, in what from our present point of view is a key statement of his thought: "Nothing is more certain, than that our manners, our civilization, and all the good things

11

which are connected with manners and with civilization have, in this European world of ours, depended for ages upon two principles; and were indeed the result of both combined; I mean the spirit of a gentleman, and the spirit of religion."

The ascendant class, therefore, and more particularly the aristocracy, comes to represent an ideal authority, expressed in the term "gentleman," at the point in history at which its effective temporal authority had begun to decline (though of course its privileges and much of its prestige remained for another century). The social function of the aristocracy has always included the art of putting on a show, of dramatizing a way of life. It is natural that America, with no hereditary aristocracy as such, should have invented an *ad hoc* aristocracy out of its entertainers, who attract much the same kind of identification that royal figures do in British countries. In the thought of Carlyle, who has no interest in spiritual authority distinct from temporal authority, and wants only to identify the two, the reactivating of the aristocracy naturally occupies a central place. For Carlyle the "holiness" or radiance of the indwelling divinity in man, which is perceptible in the hero, is the source of an undifferentiated authority which is spiritual and temporal at once.

Yet even Carlyle distinguished the *de jure* authority of the aristocracy from the *de facto* authority of captains of industry and self-made heroes of the Napoleon and Cromwell category. The basis of the distinction seems to be that as *de facto* or temporal authority is essentially active, so *de jure* or spiritual authority has something about it associated with the contemplative. In his chapter on symbolism in *Sartor Resartus* Carlyle sees the heroic personality as an "intrinsic" symbol (that is, one that has value in itself, as distinct from the flag or the cross which are extrinsic and have value only as indicators). As a symbol, the hero is the focus of a community, and the purely *le jure* figure seems to have the most prestige as one. Crowds gather to see the Queen in order to see their own unity as a society reflected in her. Here again there is a link between the recognition of spiritual authority and the dramatic function of an ascendant class.

Samuel Butler also associates spiritual authority with the aristocracy, in a more speculative and paradoxical way. He is, of course, particularly fascinated by the working of the evolutionary process in human society, and his conception of education, traditional as it is in itself, reflects this interest. He points out in *Life and Habit* that no skill is learned thoroughly until it passes through consciousness into the unconscious. It follows that the most profoundly educated people are those who have been born to wealth, leisure, and privilege, and have never been troubled by a conscious idea, which includes a good many of the aristocracy. Thus in *The Way of All Flesh* the hero, Ernest Pontifex, at that time engaged in social work in East London, meets an old classmate named Towneley who is large, handsome, simple-minded, well to do, and altogether admirable. Ernest asks Towneley effusively if he doesn't love the poor: Towneley says no, and gets away as quickly as possible. It could hardly be a briefer encounter, but it is an epiphany for Ernest: spiritual authority has spoken, as unmistakably as it spoke from the burning bush. Ernest considers this situation carefully, and finally decides: "I see it all now. The people like Towneley are the only ones who know anything that is worth knowing, and like that of course I can never be. But to make Towneleys possible, there must be hewers of wood and drawers of water—men, in fact, through whom conscious knowledge must pass before it can reach those who can apply it gracefully and instinctively as the Towneleys can."

We are reminded of the respect paid in *Erewhon* to those who are handsome, healthy, and rich, and how

13

Erewhon considers it a crime to be ill or unfortunate. I Huxley's terms, society's sympathies are with natur rather than with ethics, even though society itself is a ethical creation. Yet Ernest's solution is still a trifle in mature, and *Erewhon* brings us a little closer to Butler real view of spiritual authority. Most of the Erewhonian according to Butler, are unthinking, instinctive conserv tives, whose values are determined entirely by habit an prejudice: worshippers, as he says, of the goddess Ydgru But there is also in Erewhon a small group of "hig Ydgrunites," whom the narrator describes as the best peo ple he met in Erewhon. Of them he says: "They wer gentlemen in the full sense of the word; and what has on not said in saying this?" The high Ydgrunite would b something like Montaigne, presumably: able to live i and with society, able to see not only the power but th real significance of convention and prejudice, yet remai ing intellectually detached from them. Such gentleme are not only the natural aristocracy but the genuine apos tles of society, correcting instinct by reason and reaso by instinct, and never allowing the two to make that fat alliance which is the mark of all bigots, whether reaction ary or revolutionary.

The problem of spiritual authority, we see, has as it crucial point the problem of defining the community o such an authority. The writers we have been quoting, a of whom are deeply conservative, associate this communi ty with the ideal aristocracy which the term "gentleman' conveys. For a revolutionary thinker, such as Willian Morris, spiritual authority would be isolated from society confined to the small conspiratorial group of those wh repudiate its values and are shut out from its benefits. I is perhaps worth noting that Morris's revolutionary ideal as outlined in the future Utopia depicted in *News from Nowhere*, is the assimilating of the conception of a natura aristocracy to the whole of society. In *News from Nowhere* everybody has the creative versatility and the *sprezzature*

14

...at are the marks of the ideally educated courtier in ...astiglione, except that, of course, there is no court and ...o prince, and no one to serve except one another. They ...re at once producers and consumers, and as consumers ...hey have the sharply limited and defined quality of a ...rivileged class. "We know what we want," says one of ...hem, "so we make no more than we want." This applies ...ven to the production of human beings: the population ...as become stabilized, apparently, because people are no ...onger rutting out of nervous instability, as they do in so- ...ieties based on exploitation. The curiously childlike qual- ...y of Morris's ideal citizens is also significant, for of ...ourse the real natural aristocracy, the society of those ...ho are genuinely entitled to leisure and privilege and ...onsuming the goods produced for them by others, are ...he children.

We have just traced a parabola from the counter- ...evolutionary polemic of the later Burke to the revo- ...ationary polemic of Morris. The former places spiritual ...uthority in the middle of the ascendant class, or at least ...s center of gravity is to be found there, and the *Appeal* ...*om the New to the Old Whigs* ends in contemptuous ...dicule of John Ball, "that reverend patriarch of sedition," ...ho could not find the conception of "gentleman" in the ...riginal producing society when Adam delved and Eve ...pan. Morris, in contrast, places spiritual authority for his ...wn time in the small alienated group who are possessed ...y the ambition of realizing the dream of John Ball. For ...Morris the Peasants' Revolt was the one brief moment ...hen something like a proletariat appears in British his- ...ory. In the thought of John Stuart Mill the problem of ...piritual authority is located in a much less simplified view ...f society. For Mill, Burke's continuum of habit and ...rejudice is the way in which the majority of people live. ...eing a majority, they are not confined to a single class, ...nd the progress of democracy involves making their will ...he source of *temporal* authority. As in Burke and Butler,

15

their motivation is instinctive and empirical. Over against them are the smaller group of the liberal opposition, a much more highly individualized group, of whom Mill says that they initiate all wise and noble things.

Mill, somewhat unexpectedly, resembles Hegel in seeing the political opposition of Conservative and Liberal as the symbol of an ideal or intellectual opposition of conservative and liberal attitudes. As the liberal opposition is intellectually always a minority, it has the peculiar problem of getting enough mass support to be effective in democratic election. Some of Mill's devices, such as plurality of votes for the educated, are sufficiently desperate to indicate that this is a matter of some difficulty. To grasp the nature of the ideal opposition we have to grasp two principles. First, the majority is always right, for the majority is the source of temporal authority. Second, the majority is always wrong, for it is not the source of spiritual authority. The latter is to be found in the intellectual opposition, for "almost all the greatest men who ever lived have formed part of such an Opposition."

Authority in its two forms, therefore, rests on a paradoxical and illogical tension between majority rule and minority right. The minority are not a class but an elite, and no social epithet like "gentleman" will apply to them. In practice most of them may be gentlemen, but that is not why they belong there. The gentleman behaves according to a social convention, and for Mill the toleration of unconventional or eccentric behavior is the mark of a mature society. What holds this elite together is something intellectual, though it is certainly not intellectual agreement. To put the question in another way, what gives a minority a right? Criminals are a minority, but clearly have no right to be criminals. In the *Essay on Liberty* the right appears to be the ability to contribute something to the area of free thought and discussion which for Mill is the real parliament of man, the ideological de-

16

ate that is close to being the source of spiritual authority ecause it supplies the vision for temporal power. To permit freedom of thought is to direct freedom of action, as unrestricted speculation is the best check so far discovered on premature, spasmodic, or panic-stricken action. Here again we run into a Hegelian element in Mill's thought: no idea contributed to this social debate has any real effectiveness unless it contains its own opposite: unless, therefore, the possibility of refuting it is also present. Mill draws our attention to the peculiar importance of Rousseau in challenging the validity of the structure of society itself.

Burke's counter-revolutionary argument was based on completely inductive conception of political action; Mill's argument attempts to associate his liberal opposition with more deductive point of view. He remarks for example that "the non-existence of an acknowledged first principle has made ethics not so much a guide as a consecration of men's actual sentiments." The Utilitarian philosophy held its loyalty because it provided a major premise for majority behavior. That people will seek what they consider pleasure and avoid what they consider pain is individually probable and statistically certain. But this purely descriptive principle supplies no standard or value, no way even of distinguishing reality from illusion in the conception of pleasure. In Milton, who in *Areopagitica* presents similar conception of truth as something arrived at dynamically through the conflict of opinion, the major premises come from scripture. Milton never conceived the possibility of a free society trying to find truth without the aid of scripture. In Mill there is no clear source of the premises of debate of this kind, no set of standards and assumptions that can be taken as given. The absence of such a source may be one reason for his curious attraction toward the most uncongenial types of political dogmatists, including Carlyle and Comte (it would take us too far afield to apply this principle to Harriet Taylor),

17

as though he felt that they held some missing piece he was looking for.

In Newman, on the other hand, the source of spiritual authority is the church catholic: his great strength as a nineteenth-century thinker lay in his unvarying acceptance of that view. At no time in his adult life was Newman ever anything that a Protestant would call a Protestant: his problem was only to decide whether the Anglican or the Roman communion was the genuinely catholic one. He takes our present argument a step further by finding the road to spiritual authority through education. Education for him is partly social and retains the social aim of producing the "gentleman" which we met in Burke and Butler. Even its intellectual characteristic, a disinterested or liberal quality in it which is "its own end," has an analogy with the social ideal which is detachable from the necessity of earning a living. On its intellectual side liberal education is essentially a discipline of reason, as in Milton, and, as in Mill, it seems to have something to do with a "master view of things," a deductive or synoptic sense of intellectual form which gets one's head above the habit of living: "The principle of real dignity in Knowledge, its worth, its desirableness, considered irrespectively of its results, is this germ within it of a scientific or a philosophical process. This is how it comes to be an end in itself; this is why it admits of being called Liberal."

But the university turns out to be a function of the church, and the education it gives confronts the student with a dilemma: he must either attach himself along with his education to the church or keep his education as a private possession. Recurrently we have come to this point of having to define the community of spiritual authority. The individual can readily be seen to be capable of understanding more than society in general, and hence of possessing standards and values, with an authority superior in kind if not in power. But the conception

18

gentleman," however interpreted, defines the superior individual rather than the superior group, even granted that one may recognize the individual as one of a group. For Newman only the church provides this community, and of the gentlemen who cannot commit themselves to he says: "When they do wrong, they feel, not contrition, of which God is the object, but remorse, and a sense of degradation. . . . They are victims of an intense self-contemplation."

In Newman's view of the church there is no place, as here would have to be in Protestant thinkers, including Milton, for a dialogue between scripture and church. The church for Newman is the definitive teacher of doctrine; hence it encloses scripture, and operates on ordinary society very much as the British constitution does in Burke. For Burke the conflict of classes and their interests, in free society, is settled by a legal compromise which preserves the rights of both parties, and these compromises then form a series of precedents diffusing freedom through society, as the quarrels of king and barons produced Magna Carta and the quarrels of king and Parliament the Bill of Rights. Newman sees church doctrine as developing in a somewhat similar way, being evolved out of the crises of history, defining a dogma here, marking off a heresy there, in an endless pilgrimage toward the City of God. Thus spiritual authority in Newman is, as in Milton, a revelation, but a revelation that has no place for metamorphosis, for the revolutionary and apocalyptic transformation of society.

In Arnold, the conception "culture" is the basis from which we have to start. In using the phrase "spiritual authority" to describe a pervasive problem of nineteenth-century thought, I have been putting unfamiliar conceptions into the minds of some of my writers. For Mill, the problem is not exactly one of *spiritual* authority, and for Butler, it is not exactly a problem of authority. But Ar-

19

nold is quite explicit about the authoritative nature of culture: "If we look at the world outside us we find a disquieting absence of sure authority. We discover that only in right reason can we get a source of sure authority and culture brings us towards right reason." The traditional elements of gentleman and liberal education are both involved in Arnold's culture, but Arnold clears up a point about the social location of spiritual authority that has been confusing us so far. We noticed that the more conservative a writer is, the more inclined he is to locate spiritual authority in the middle of actual society, in the place of greatest prestige and prominence. The more radical he is, the more inclined he is to locate it in an opposition, an alien or even excluded group. Something in Arnold—possibly the Romantic poet in him—realizes that the center is the place of greatest isolation. The argument of *Culture and Anarchy* is to the effect that what is of greatest cultural value, such as a university or the established church, is central to society and demands to be placed at the center, in the position of Carlyle's intrinsic symbol. Society itself presents a conflict of class interests and culture for Arnold operates like law in Burke or doctrine in Newman, as a harmonizing principle creating a new kind of order out of this conflict. Those who support it have to begin by isolating themselves from class conflict, which means isolating themselves from the present structure of society: "Within each of these classes there are a certain number of *aliens,* if we may so call them,—persons who are mainly led, not by their class spirit, but by a general *humane* spirit, by the love of human perfection."

Culture represents an evaluation—the *best* that has been thought and said—and the conception of "best" is bound up with permanence. Class conflict deals with temporary issues, and its arguments are rationalizations based on a temporary situation. Temporal power is based on the ascendancy of one class—here we come back to Milon's conception of temporal power as an interim power. The class qua class is always anticultural: the aristocracy, considered purely as a class, are only barbarians, the middle class only Philistines, the lower class only a populace. Hence it would be the wildest paradox to think of creating a new society through the dictatorship of one class. It is culture that is the genuinely revolutionary force in society, for culture "seeks to do away with classes," and tends to create out of actual society an ideal order of liberty, equality, and fraternity. Culture for Arnold is a whole of which the church forms part, but as culture is not, like church, the name of a specific community, the problem of defining the community of spiritual authority is still with us.

The question of the origin of spiritual authority, and of whether that origin is purely human, partly human, or wholly superhuman has come up at various times in this inquiry. Anyone working out this question in Christian terms, whether Catholic or Protestant, would be likely to say that its origin is out of human reach, though the fact that Christ is at once God, Man, and Logos guarantees the validity of human reason as a means of receiving it, at least up to a point. For Burke and Butler, in different ways, spiritual authority, or whatever is homologous with it, comes to us as a process of nature, a datum or something given, which we may modify but must first of all accept. We have seen that spiritual authority begins in the recognition of truth, and truth usually has about it some quality of the objective, something presented to us. But for a liberal thinker, such as Mill, there can hardly be any real spiritual authority apart from what man himself creates. A revolutionary thinker would go a step further and see in truth itself a human creation which, as man continues to create it, he may also re-create. Marx's second thesis on Feuerbach makes this quite clear: "The question whether objective truth can be attributed to human thinking is not a question of theory, but is a prac-

21

tical question. In practice man must prove the truth, that is, the reality and power, the this-sidedness of his thinking." Arnold's "culture" unites these qualities of the datum and the continuous creation, being a human construct which, so far as it is rooted in the past, possesses an objective authority. This authority, we should note, is not exclusively intellectual, for "many things are not seen in their true nature and as they really are, unless they are seen as beautiful," and the imagination as well as the reason may recognize a monument of its own magnificence.

Wherever we turn in nineteenth-century thought we meet some version of a "drunken boat" construct, where the values of humanity, intelligence, or cultural and social tradition keep tossing precariously in a sort of Noah's ark on top of a menacing and potentially destructive force. This is the relation of the world as idea to the world as will in Schopenhauer, of ethics to evolution in Darwin and Huxley, of the ascendant class to the proletariat in Marx, and, later, of ego to libido and id in Freud. There are also many variants of a "saving remnant" theory, ranging from Coleridge's "clerisy" to various pleas for a new kind of monastic movement (one thinks of the symbolic function of the idealized monastery in the argument of Carlyle's *Past and Present*). Of other metaphors of spiritual authority, two are conspicuous. One is the metaphor of the social human body, whose seat of intelligence and authority ought to be somewhere on top, as it is in the individual body. The other is the thermostat or feedback metaphor which has organized so much social thinking in the last two centuries. In a sense the search for spiritual authority is really the search for a "governor" in the mechanical sense, something that distributes the rhythm of a mechanism without being involved in the mechanism itself. This figure appears in Huxley's *Evolution and Ethics*: "To this extent the general cosmic process begins to be checked by a rudimentary ethical process, which is, strictly speaking, part of the former, just as the 'governor' in a steam engine is part of the mechanism of the engine."

The problem dealt with in this paper could of course be extended over a far wider area of nineteenth-century thought than I am here able to cover. So far as I know, the twentieth century has not added much to the question, which may be one reason why the political axioms and assumptions of the twentieth century are still rooted in the nineteenth. It seems to me, however, appropriate for an audience celebrating a step in the progress of a university to consider whether the university itself may not have a peculiarly close relationship to the question. In particular, the university seems to me to come closer than any other human institution to defining the community of spiritual authority. Newman's view that the university is a function of the church, with theology occupying a central role as the queen of sciences, does not seem to be borne out by the development of universities in the last century. I have no doubt that religion indicates where the ultimate source of spiritual authority is, nor that the churches have an essential function as custodians and interpreters of its tradition. But in the present-day shape of society, so dominated by science and technology, they clearly have only a partial and peripheral role in embodying the spiritual authority of that society.

Arnold comes nearest to seeing the universities in this light, but universities in his day, and more particularly as he conceived them, made it necessary for him to distinguish them from "culture." A century later, we seem to be living our lives on two levels. One is the level of ordinary society, which is in so constant a state of revolution and metamorphosis that it cannot be accepted as the real form of human society at all, but only as the transient appearance of real society. Real society itself can only be the world revealed to us through the study of the arts and sciences, the total body of human achievement out of which the forces come that change ordinary society so rapidly. Of this world the universities are the social embodiment, and they represent what seems to me today the only visible direction in which our higher loyalties and obligations can go.

Walter J. Ong, S.J.

NEWMAN'S ESSAY ON DEVELOPMENT

IN ITS INTELLECTUAL MILIEU

An Essay on the Development of Christian Doctrine is the central point in Newman's intellectual and religious career. [1] Written in his last days as an Anglican and published immediately after his entrance into the Church, the *Essay on Development* not only stands at the crossroads to mark where Newman's thought turns squarely onto the Catholic highway, but also serves as a meeting point where his earlier historical studies and theological theories converge and reach their fulfillment. [2] As Newman's studies had matured, the *Essay on Development* had been more and more immanent in his thought: indeed, it was already more than immanent when the sermon entitled "The Theory of Developments in Religious Doctrine" culminated Newman's Oxford preaching in 1843. [3]

Besides being immanent in his earlier work, the *Essay on Development* is also the point from which grows the work of Newman's later years. Thus, from its middle position in Newman's intellectual history, it faces both ways to give this history a unified significance. This is plain

---

This study, abridged here, appeared originally in *Theological Studies*, VII (1946), 3-45.

from Newman's habitual way of viewing his own acti‹
ities. Newman's life work, reduced to its simplest term‹
presented itself to his own mind as a struggle against li‹
eralism or the anti-dogmatic principle. [4] In this strugg‹
the *Essay on Development* occupies the key positio‹
When, for example, toward the close of his life, in a lett‹
to his friend the arch-liberal, arch-positivist Willia‹
Froude, Newman seeks to define his anti-liberal positio‹
he quotes from the *University Sermons* to represent h‹
early thought, from the *Grammar of Assent* [5] to represe‹
his late thought, and from the *Essay on Development* ‹
link the early and the late periods. [6]

Newman's thought has an importance beyond that ‹
the thought of an individual man. In *La philosophie ‹
Newman,* M. Jean Guitton has pointed out that Newma‹
like St. Augustine, perceived that his own personal cris‹
was the same as that of the entire world. [7] Father Eric‹
Przywara has made much the same point. [8] The respo‹
sive mind of Newman was certainly one of the most se‹
sitive gauges on which the intellectual movements of th‹
age registered themselves. The interests which always po‹
sessed him, he tells us in the *Apologia,* were things whic‹
were "in the air." [9] At the Oxford in which his thoug‹
matured, the party of which Newman was the "life an‹
soul" [10] had an appeal so deep-rooted in the intellectu‹
world of which Oxford was the center that William Georg‹
Ward's "Credo in Newmannum" became a partisan ra‹
lying cry. [11] Indeed, touching the livest issues at Oxfor‹
at their deepest quick, the interests to which Newman an‹
those around him were dedicated finally split open th‹
University's entire intellectual front. [12] Newman's thoug‹
was radically that of the commonwealth of mind of th‹
England of his day. This was the nineteenth-century worl‹
which reached back to the purlieus of the Anglican divine‹
Bull, Taylor, Law, and most of all Butler, and which als‹
was of a piece with the world of Hume and Kant an‹
Hegel.

Another figure who might be singled out besides Newman as thoroughly representative of this world is Coleridge. Indeed, almost no figure is more representative. And Newman's own representative quality is attested to by his immediate response to the earlier writer: "During this spring [1835] I for the *first time* read parts of Coleridge's works; and I am surprised how much I thought mine, is to be found there." [13]

The mind of Newman, so representative of that of his age, had itself an individual history which can be described as an increasingly intimate contact with revelation. Newman writes:

When I was fifteen (in the autumn of 1816), a great change of thought took place in me. I fell under the influences of a definite Creed, and received into my intellect impressions of dogma, which, through God's mercy, have never been effaced or obscured. Above and beyond the conversations and sermons of the excellent man, long dead, the Rev. Walter Mayers, of Pembroke College, Oxford, who was the human means of this beginning of divine faith in me, was the effect of the books which he put into my hands, all of the school of Calvin. [14]

This initial contact with revelation was strengthened and given shape at Oxford, as Newman, increasingly aware of the issues at stake between revealed, dogmatic religion and liberalism, adhered to the "High Church" party of Keble. [15] His migration from Keble's side to the Catholic position was simply an advance along the same route which he had taken to join Keble. As Newman himself explains, it was none other than Keble who, in his Assize Sermon of 1833 published under the title "National Apostasy," drew the lines of the dogmatic-liberal dispute in such a way as to start the movement which ultimately led Newman into the Church. [16]

At the point where this mind, filled with the ways of thinking of its age, arrived at the complete Catholic acceptance of revelation, stands the *Essay on Development*.

Newman had grown up into Evangelical Protestar ism, [17] which ingenuously scouted questions of develo ment of dogma, assuming that everything it said could found verbatim in the Scriptures. From this Evangelica ism Newman had been turned, at the sharp point of fac into the Anglican camp. But here he found that, whe put to the test, the Anglican tradition itself fell back take what was essentially a Protestant stand. For the mo part, the primitive Anglicans of the sixteenth and seve teenth centuries had not, indeed, like the Evangelic Protestants, ejected the Roman "corruptions" from the teachings: they had found themselves in dispute wi Rome principally on matters of jurisdiction. [18] But by h day, as Newman discovered to his chagrin, the leaders the Anglican Church required a Protestant interpretatic of the Thirty-Nine Articles [19]—an interpretation whic the history of these articles plainly showed to be qui unwarranted. [20]

There were many in the Anglican Church who retaine interest in dogma. These were the ones who had given th church its appeal to Newman. But even these were fine ing in experience, what they may not yet have been awa of in theory, that without a Holy See they had no pra ticable mechanism to guarantee the validity of any de velopment in doctrine, and that, since the Anglican Churc therefore could not speak with confidence of any deve opment now within its own teaching, it had to deny tha any development had ever taken place in Christian doc trine. In this sense, when they were put to the test an made to formulate their position, the only tenable refug for Anglicans came eventually to be in practice quite lik that of the Evangelical Protestants. [21] Except for those whom doctrine meant little or nothing—those, for i stance, who in the spirit of true dogmatic Whiggery pr jected the Jerusalem bishopric negotiations so repugnar

28

Newman and the other defenders of dogma [22]—Anglicans took the position that the doctrine of the Anglican Church, word for word, corresponded, not precisely to the Gospels (here indeed was a hopeful difference with the Evangelicals) but to the doctrine of the Church of the first centuries. [23] This view did not assume that everything was in the Scriptures; it allowed for tradition. But it did assume that the Christianity of the first centuries was static, at least as static as the Anglican doctrine, which had nothing to do now with new definitions of popes or councils. This is the position which Newman found himself taking when he proposed his doctrine of the "Via Media" in expounding the Thirty-Nine Articles. [24]

But as Newman gained greater familiarity with the Christianity of the early centuries, and particularly as he studied the Monophysite controversies, [25] he found many difficulties. They all came to this: between the Christianity of the Gospels and the Christianity even of Chalcedon, there were already differences. [26] Wherever you found Christianity in the early centuries, you found not a static, but a developing doctrine. [27] In other words, early Christianity was behaving in a way suspiciously like Rome's way of behaving. [28] The Council of Chalcedon, which the Anglicans accepted, was only an earlier Council of Trent, and Trent they did not accept.

The *Essay on Development* may be summarized as an explanation with illustrations: an explanation of how natural "ideas," to use Newman's own term, grow or develop over a long course of time when they are the possession of many men, with elaborate illustrations of how the apparent doctrinal differences between primitive Christianity and the Roman Catholic Church of the nineteenth century can be explained as the same sort of development. The natural "ideas" to which Newman compares the development of Christianity are such "ideas" as Platonic philosophy, or the doctrine of the divine right of kings,

29

or the duty of benevolent enterprises, or utilitarianis
or the doctrine of the rights of man, or of free trade,
of the anti-social bearings of a priesthood, and so on.

How are such "ideas" psychologically constituted? Ne
man refuses to commit himself on this. [30] He merely ava
himself of illustrations. [31] He notes, for example, amo
other things, that the English Parliament of 1628-16
took a series of measures without suggesting that th
all flowed from a common source. [32] Newman is appa
ently referring to the passage of the Petition of Rig
which provided that there should be no more taxati
without the consent of parliament, no more billeting
soldiers in private houses, no more martial law in time
peace, and no more imprisonment without a specifi
charge. But after twelve years, says Newman, the Lo
Parliament found itself stripping the monarch of some
his power. The idea of a more limited monarchy now f
the first time was explicitly invoked. But this "idea" ha
been operating for twelve years. This is typical of the
lustrations outside Christianity which Newman suppli
as parallels to doctrinal development in the Church.

Newman next turns to Christian doctrine and shows th
similar phenomena are found there. Thus, on the doctri
of papal supremacy, the clearly developed teaching of t
fourth century is an "idea" which had always been wor
ing in the ferment of Christian life, but which only nc
rose to the surface. [33] Newman elaborates many other e
amples of doctrinal development, and in the latter ha
of the *Essay on Development* simply vindicates vario
Catholic developments as true developments and not cc
ruptions.

Thus the *Essay on Development* is laid out in this rou
plan: There exist on the natural level certain central
root "ideas" which develop; Christianity does likewis
the latter point is confirmed by sundry examples.

How would one state the "leading idea" or the "ro

a" of any one of those phenomena just listed above, to
ich Newman compares Christianity? Newman, as has
t been seen, refers to these phenomena themselves as
eas", [34] and if we follow this practice of his, we would
the present question this way: How would one state
"leading idea" or the "root idea" of any one of these
as—Platonic philosophy, the doctrine of the divine
ht of kings, and so on? That is to say, how would one
equately formulate or conceptualize any of these ideas
which Christianity is compared? How, for instance,
uld one so formulate or conceptualize what we call
atonism? Is it that a notional world exists *a parte rei?*
that what is mutable cannot be real or true? Or that
spiritual and the material are completely separated?

These, and any other formulations of Platonism, would
ch be in Newman's view inadequate. We cannot, he
ys, "inclose in a formula that intellectual fact, or sys-
m of thought, which we call the Platonic philosophy,
that historical phenomenon of doctrine and conduct,
ich we call the heresy of Montanus or of Manes." [35]
e adequate "idea" of Platonism is "commensurate with
sum total of its possible aspects, however they may
ry in the separate consciousness of individuals." [36] There
no "leading idea" separate from this totality. What are
lled "leading ideas" of Platonism or utilitarianism or
other such things are only partial glimpses, for the idea
Platonism and the ideas of the other similar phenom-
a which Newman enumerates are like bodily substances
ich admit "of being walked round, and surveyed on
posite sides, and in different perspectives, and in con-
ry lights, in evidence of their reality." [37] The one truth
ich shows up only partially in each one of the partial
impses is what Newman calls the "idea" in the adequate
complete sense; this is the idea which develops.

Similarly, on the supernatural plane, Newman will not
sign the "central idea'" of Christianity any more than

31

he will the central idea of Platonism, but he says that f
convenience one can take the Incarnation. [38] God becon
Man. Looked at as both God and Man, then, Christ stan
between our Creator and us, and we have the doctrine
mediation and the hierarchy, which is one aspect of Chr
tianity. Or again, the divine has established a special
rect contact with our material world; this gives us t
sacramental system, another aspect. Or again, there is t
doctrine of the kenosis, and we have Christian asceticis
Newman bases these three important aspects of Chris
anity on the Incarnation. But no one of them, nor ev
the Incarnation itself, is the "central idea" of Christiani
the idea of Christianity. [39]

In his refusal to say what is the central idea of Chr
tianity Newman assigns his reason, and it is a reas
which is connected with the natural "ideas" to which
compares Christianity: any one statement of Christian
would be inadequate because even in the natural order
one statement which man can make will exhaust a truth.
Thus, when the all-important question underlying his bo
is broached, and Newman asks *what* is developed in Chr
tian doctrine, he handles the question by referring to
analogy between the natural and the supernatural. T
fact is of some importance, as we shall see.

NEWMAN AND BISHOP BUTLER

The analogy of which Newman here avails himself h
for him a definite context. When Newman was a you
man, he had read the book by the eighteenth-century A
glican bishop, Joseph Butler, *The Analogy of Religio
Natural and Revealed, to the Constitution and Course
Nature,* [41] which is quoted so often in the *Essay on D
velopment.* Butler's is undoubtedly the most pervasive i
fluence which any one writer ever exercised on Newma
and to Butler he explicitly credits his own awareness

analogy between the natural and the supernatural—
a analogy which, Newman points out, is at the base of
that he calls the "sacramental" view of the universe—
together with another equally basic principle of his
thought, that of probability as a guide of life. [42] Newman's
consuming enthusiasm for the early Fathers was connected with his perception of something like this "sacramental"
view of Butler's in the various "economies" or "dispensa-
tions" of eternal Truth, of which these Fathers speak.

In his *Analogy,* a famous book in its day, and one
whose influence on English thought can still be marked,
Butler had set himself against the deists, who claimed to
judge revelation by natural reason but *de facto* demanded
of revelation what they never found in nature: that it be
clear-cut, that it conform to previous expectations, that
its choice of means to achieve its ends be just what man
would expect on a *prima facie* examination, and so on.
Butler's attack on this mentality is simple: examine the
real world as it is known from experience, not an ima-
ginary world, and you will find that revelation works just
as the real world does. [43] Both are mysterious, both full
of obscurities, both unpredictable and unintelligible except at the expense of great effort—the parallels carry out
in many directions and with remarkable detail. Arguing
in this fashion, Butler seeks to defend revelation by calling for a revised, more factual view of natural reality.
His *Analogy* sets about pointing out details of the faulty
view and illustrating how revelation conforms to the real,
the true view based on the facts as we have them. The
Analogy does not concern itself with the particular problems of revelation at all. Indeed, Butler is so eminently
concerned with the natural that he tends throughout the
treatise to minimize the effect of the revelation of *myster-
ia stricte dicta;* he does not conceive of revelation as part
of an economy of an elevated human nature. His super-
naturalism in the *Analogy* appears rather like a naturalism grown somewhat gigantesque. [44]

33

Equipped with the lesson he had learned as a yout
from Butler, that revelation follows nature, Newman b
came gradually aware, as we have seen, of the proble
of doctrinal development. Now that his eyes were opene
he thought: nature develops; why not expect somethir
analogous in revelation? Dogma, although it be reveale
is expressed in terms with natural origins, and so it mu
partake somewhat of the properties of these terms. Indee
Butler himself had already touched explicitly, if light
and briefly, on the question of development. [45]

When Newman falls back on the analogy that revel:
tion acts as nature acts, the question can well be aske
whether he analyzes his opponents' difficulties exactly :
Butler had analyzed his opponents'—whether he decid
that Protestant difficulties against Catholic doctrines a
based on a faulty view of natural reality. To answer th
question we must examine Newman's argument in term
of the general views of natural reality current in his da

NEWMAN'S DIFFERENCE WITH HIS OPPONENTS

Newman not only exploits in the *Essay on Developmen*
the analogy between the supernatural and the natural, b
also utilizes other sorts of analogies to elucidate the n:
ture of development in "ideas" on the natural plane. C
all the means he uses to bring out what occurs in that d
velopment of natural ideas to which he compares the d
velopment of Christian doctrine, the means which bull
largest in point of space and importance is the analog
with organic life. Once Newman has, in his Introductio
cleared a preliminary gangway through his adversaries f
the movement of his own thought, the analogy with o
ganic life comes immediately to the front and, from th
first chapter on, remains prominent throughout the boo

Thus, the idea is "propagated" after the fashion of m:
terial living things. Its development is initially described i

34

rganic terms as "the germination and maturation of ome truth or apparent truth on a large mental field." [46] This implies two correlates: first, germination and maturation in the individual, and secondly, germination and maturation in the community or aggregate of individuals.

The analogy with organic life runs throughout the *Essay on Development*. Analogously with material things, he "idea" which is capable of developing has in its own way, as we have seen, even something like parts outside of parts—various "aspects" which are explained by Newman as being "mutually connected and growing one out of another." [47] The question is raised whether in the intellect of the reader the ideas latent in written documents "open out . . . and grow to perfection in the course of time." [48] They do. Moreover, the idea of Christianity considered as an "idea" in the natural sense, the supernatural qualities being prescinded from) not only grows "in wisdom and stature," but it even has a nativity, though it be a miraculous one. [49] Further, even if we were to suppose that revelation were not given to man by stages, so that it thus developed in a way resembling growth, but rather that it came in full maturity from God's hand as plants did in creation (according to Newman's interpretation of Genesis), it would nevertheless, like plants, need propagation; it would have to be conveyed to uninspired minds. [50]

Further elucidations in terms of organic life occur throughout the *Essay on Development*, [51] and all need not be retailed here. Indeed, Part II of the *Essay on Development*, the entire latter two-thirds of the book, rests as a whole directly on the analogy with organic life. Entitled "Doctrinal Developments Viewed Relatively to Doctrinal Corruptions," it faces squarely the standard Protestant and Anglican charge that Roman Catholicism had corrupted the primitive Faith or the primitive "idea" of Christianity. The very notion of corruption is applicable

35

only to material things, and, as Newman further argues, in the sense in which the term "corruption" is employed in the familiar indictment of Catholicism, it refers to the kind of corruption peculiar to *living* material beings. [52] In other words, this very indictment is based, unwittingly perhaps, on the analogy between the primitive "idea" of Christianity and a living organism. Newman's refutation of it is based on the implications of the analogy: if a thing corrupts in the way a living material being corrupts, it must have the power of development which is the correlative of corruption in such a being.

By making so much of the analogy with organic life in explaining the development of an idea, Newman puts into the reader's hands the principal clue to what lies back of his point that no one statement which man can make will exhaust an "idea." For Newman is not saying simply that the idea is alive or that it is material. It acts as only a thing can act which participates in *both* life and matter.

From this point on, there opens a large field of questions at the base of Newman's discussion, and it is plain that they are not strictly theological questions, but philosophical questions which open onto theology. This brings out an important matter. In the *Essay on Development* there is not a word about the special problems which the development of supernatural revelation raises, nothing about the special problems of development in a cognition so especially close to the divine, so especially unified as is supernatural revelation compared with natural cognition, no attempt to explain the relations and differences between the way the human mind holds natural truths and the way it holds supernatural mysteries. There is much about the development of ideas, but not a word about anything distinctive of the development of revelation.

Newman had set out to argue against Evangelical Protestants and Anglicans, both of whom theoretically ased their religious views on revelation, but we do not find him joining issue with them primarily on the ground of the content of revelation. We do not find one side maintaining that revelation says this and the other side maintaining that it says that, after the fashion of most parties to disputes over revealed doctrine. It is not a question of what God says, but of what His deposited doctrine does; and Newman urges his case by calling on the opposition to take a fuller view of natural reality. Protestants and Anglicans err by making the deposit of revelation behave in a way in which no possession of the human mind can behave. [53]

Thus, to answer our earlier question, Newman is doing no more than Butler had done in telling his adversaries that they impose on revelation their false notions of natural reality. His discussion is merely more particularized than Butler's. In place of Butler's recommendation of a more adequate general awareness of the "order and course of nature" as a corrective for a general misapprehension of supernatural truth, Newman recommends an awareness of the development of natural "ideas," and in particular an awareness of the material component in human intellection, largely as brought out by the analogy between human intellection and organic life. Our knowledge is both in material being and directed primarily to material being. It is never pure intellection any more than we are ever pure spirits.

The tradition in Newman's world which regarded human intellection as pure intellection is not far to seek. It is that idealism which constitutes a persistent aberration of human thought but which descends to Newman's age proximately through Descartes, Hume, Kant, and Hegel. [54] The *Essay on Development* is an opposition to this tradition, based on particular grounds—namely, as the facts connected with the history of revelation. The great treatise thus resolves itself into a struggle between the idealist's view of human intellection and an opposed view based, as we believe, on more complete and accurate reporting of facts. This resolution helps place the treatise in Newman's intellectual milieu. For the *Essay on Development,* as we have seen, marks a stage in the journey of a highly representative mind coming into fuller and fuller contact with revelation; and the stage it marks is the one at which this mind, accepting revelation now unconditionally, turns to face the forces opposed to revelation. The fact that when it does this it finds itself facing the idealistic tradition identifies this tradition as the great force on which the anti-dogmatism of the day was relying, and establishes the position of the *Essay on Development* in terms of the radical opposition of Christianity to the hostile elements in the nineteenth-century milieu.

THE POSITIVIST MIND AND FIRST PRINCIPLES

Since his great intellectual foe was the anti-dogmatic mind, the mind whose bent is ordinarily diagnosed as "materialistic," it may seem strange that Newman himself should have turned to ways of thinking which so heavily underscore the connections of human intellection with the material world. What is the reason for this strange homeopathy?

The disease of the positivist mind is that, while it uses all along a method of rising from the singular fact to the universal—be this only the probable—a method of departing from matter, it tries at the same time to deny that it uses any such method at all, or indeed that any such method is ever necessary. This denial, of course, effectively scotches any attempt to use other methods. If the positivist physicist can say he considers only facts—which is sheer self-deception—he can very well ridicule the metaphysician. For the metaphysician plainly gets away from facts. Since he deals with the more abstract, it is harder for him to pretend that he does not get away rom them. The trouble is that the positivist physicist gets way from facts, too. And so does the mathematician, 1ore evidently even than the physicist. The ridicule is all ased on a hoax.

But Newman was faced with it. His long-drawn-out truggle can be viewed in close focus within the corre-pondence between himself and William Froude. Froude, 'ho developed from a young Oxford mathematician whose apers were a little beyond the depths of the junior dons 1to the great pioneer in the science of hydrodynamics, an stand as a type of the nineteenth-century mind which Iewman was trying to bring to an "enlargement of vi-ion." From Newman's entrance into the Church in 1845 ntil Froude died in 1879, still not won to the Faith, the orrespondence went on. Froude is uniformly the physi-ist insisting on his science's findings, his science's induc-ions, and the manner in which these are continually kept lose to fact. [55]

In Newman's highly significant final letter, already ited, the rough draft of which lay unfinished when news ame of Froude's death, the cardinal-elect patiently and iscerningly insists that this kind of discussion does not ind the point at issue:

My first and lasting impression is that in first principles we gree together more than you allow; and this is a difficulty in 1y meeting you, that I am not sure you know what I hold and 'hat I don't; otherwise why should [you] insist so strongly n points which I maintain as strongly as you?

Thus you insist very strongly on knowledge mainly depend-1g upon the experience of facts, as if I denied it; whereas, s a general truth and when experience is attainable, I hold t more fully than you. I say "more fully," because, whereas ou hold that "to *select,* square, and to fit together materials 'hich experience has supplied is the very function of the in-ellect," I should [not] allow the intellect to select, but only ɔ estimate them. [56]

Jewman's analysis is here wonderfully penetrating. The ɔositivist does not take *all* the facts; he selects only some.

And his selection is determined, consciously or not, by the goal he has set for himself, which is a limited goal.

Froude had made the typical mistake here. He had mistaken *a* use of facts for *the* use of facts; he had the knack of using them as the physicist does. And because it was a knack, because this knack, nothing else than a way of making an induction, was so basic a process, so elemental an item in the life of the intellect, that it could not very well be described in terms more elemental than itself, he took it for granted that it went with the facts themselves and that his particular method must always accompany the use of facts. In doing this, he, consciously or not, discards whole worlds of reality which do not fit in with his method. When he saw Newman employing another method, he took it for granted that Newman was denying to facts the kind of primacy which they should enjoy.

But Newman was, as he himself explains, only denying that facts were synonymous with Froude's method of using them. For the hydrodynamics engineer was *using* facts as truly as anyone else. He had set himself toward a goal, and he was scraping together the facts which would get him to it. This is a valid procedure for science—indeed, the only procedure possible. The scientist must know in advance whether he is gathering facts for biological or chemical or physical purposes. A random agglomeration of objectives will get him nowhere. This means that there must be selection of facts. Newman was only saying that when we are seeking to present a complete overview of reality, we have no warrant for arbitrary selection: "I should not allow the intellect to select, but only to estimate them." Although Froude's habitual exploitation of facts for the ends of physical science was a particular use determined by a particular objective, he should have seen that, with other objectives in mind, one could make facts yield additional truths.

It is quite accurate to diagnose a mind like Froude's as materialistic, if this is understood to mean that such a mind habitually restricts its operations to the levels of physical and mathematical abstractions, which lie closer to matter than the level of metaphysical science, and that such a mind is violently constraining itself to avoid even that elementary metaphysical abstraction which is a normal activity of every healthy human intellect. But it is an inaccurate diagnosis leading to a fatal prescription to maintain that such a "materialistic" mind pays too close attention to material being and makes too little of the powers of man's mind. The result of this diagnosis is to insist that the materialist put aside material being and devote himself to higher things.

This is fatal because it presupposes that man's intellectual life is divorced completely from the material. As a matter of fact, it is not.

The diagnosis which Newman's procedure implies is more discerning and promising. The materialist is not at fault for paying too close attention to material things. He pays too restricted an attention to them. He does not notice the half of what is in them. He finds in them answers to his questions, but he fails to notice the other questions which material things raise. Since the human intellect begins with the material world, from which it gets all the knowledge that it naturally acquires, the natural cure for the positivist or materialist mind is for it to examine material things more closely. The materialist's world—the material world as the materialist explains it—is not self-contained at all; for the very reality to which his explanations refer raises questions, as it provides answers, at a level beyond that of physics and mathematics.

Its practice of performing only certain types of induction not only conditions the positivist mind against metaphysics and the approach to God by natural reason, but also in a peculiar fashion conditions it against those movements by which it should come, under grace, to the possession of supernatural truth. The rule that man's intellect must start from material reality and proceed by inductions, if it is to possess truth, is applicable not only to the natural sciences, but also, in a limited and special way, to the supernatural possession of truth by the light of faith. The rule applies in this sense: the establishing of the existence of revelation, which is the ordinary preamble by which the adult mind approaches under the influence of the Holy Spirit to the act of faith, in many ways does not so much resemble a process of ratiocination—a movement which is initiated and carried through at one abstract level—as it does an induction, a movement initiated on the concrete plane.

This is, of course, not to say that the establishing of the existence of revelation is not reasonable; rather the contrary. It would be reasonable even were the parallel with induction much closer than it really is; for induction is eminently reasonable. Without induction no reasoning is possible, and it is the start of the ratiocinative process. Moreover, we know that the act of faith is an intellectual assent, and that among the steps which precede the assent of faith there are intellectual processes. But of all the things which the intellect does, ratiocination is the least perfect, and, it must be said, the least characteristic of intellect as intellect. God and the angels do not reason. A reasoned conclusion has no certainty of its own apart from that of its premises. And its premises are ultimately based on the simple intuition which is the proper work of intellect as intellect. For man, this simple intuition is best represented in the inductive process. It is hardly necessary to note that in comparing the *praeambula fidei* to an induction, we are not comparing them to a *congeries probabilitatum;* for an induction is not such a *congeries* but an operation of the intellect which intuits a universal concept or a universal judgment because the sense facul ties have provided it with sufficiently numerous instances to make possible the intuition of a universal.

The parallel between the inductive process and the steps which, under grace, precede the act of faith (in the adult convert) is of course not exact. Unlike a real induction, this process leads to a singular: "God has revealed." But it does suggest an induction in that it is a process leading to a higher level of intelligibility: beyond this preliminary term, which asserts, "God has revealed," lies Truth at a higher level than man could otherwise reach. And if all the understanding and science which man has naturally is based on induction, on ascent out of singular material things, what is more likely than that in His providence, when He comes to give a higher understanding to man, God should go about it by a process which in some way parallels the natural? This is the ordinary order of divine providence which we have learned to expect.

And thus we find that, as in a real induction, the mind being brought to the assent of faith travels a road where, at least frequently, it considers separate instances of things attesting to revelation. The steps which it takes involve the balancing and sifting of a complex of evidence, the educing of a truth from a body of separate concrete facts, each one of which, somewhat as in an induction, reflects light on the other.

Newman's interiority, his "ontologism," lies within this frame. There is hardly much room for "interior preparation" in the manipulation of a syllogism, which proceeds the same way in the science of biology as it does in geometry or anywhere else. But there is great need of interior preparation in the intellectual management of concrete facts. Thinking in this vein, Newman makes the point that the man who has more facts on hand to lead him to suspect the likelihood and the nature of revelation can recognize revelation, when it takes place, more readily than

43

the man who has never even begun to look for indications of what revelation, if it takes place, might turn out to be. [57] A parallel with the laboratory offers itself again: the technician who already has a fund of probable knowledge concerning a chemical can come to a certain and full knowledge of its reactions with the same experiments and exactly the same results which leave the novice, who has had no probable knowledge whatsoever, only uncertain and bewildered.

Newman's interiority here is, of course, complicated by the fact that some of the evidence for the likelihood, and even for the probable nature, of revelation is to be gathered from the problems which one experiences in one's own interior moral life. [58]

In the last analysis, the difficulty of the positivist mind, in so far as we can regard this difficulty while prescinding from the question of grace, is resolvable in terms of the origin of first principles. The fact that the positivist mind, in conditioning itself to certain ways of rising out of the material, has also conditioned itself against other ways, means that it has artificially stunted its operations by restricting the first principles with which it operates. Man should not so fall in love with his limited achievements as to think that there are no others. The condition in which the positivist mind here finds itself stands in the way of its acceptance of dogma or supernatural mystery, and it stands in the way even if the two preliminary hurdles—proof from reason of the existence of God and proof of revelation—are somehow cleared; for the dogmas of faith are first principles. They are first principles in the sense that they are not proved or provable in themselves, although they are indeed incontestable, arrived at legitimately—the process of getting at them can be justified—and in the sense that they do not depend on other truths but other truths on them. They differ from other first principles in the sense that they are not educed from ma-

erial things but simply *per se* supplied us by God. This
is to say that, unlike other first principles, they are not
understandable, but are mysteries.

As the positivist mind has the knack, the "feel," for
only certain kinds of induction, so it has the "feel" for
only certain kinds of first principles. The more resilient
mentality can rebound from its impact with reality to the
various levels of being, and, while it cannot achieve of its
own power the mysteries of faith, still it is used to a
variety of levels, and it is thus not so surprised, not so ill
at ease, at the possibility of a still higher level than those
to which it naturally attains. The positivist mind is more
unsettled by such a possibility; for it seeks to restrict the
levels of abstraction. If it is thereby antagonistic to the
first principles of metaphysics, it is not strange that it will
a fortiori be antagonistic to the first principles of a still
higher knowledge, or that, if it admits the truths of revelation, it will deny them the character of first principles
and will seek to kill off the science of theology because
theology insists on taking them as such. [59]

It becomes evident at this point that his insistence on
the value of a liberal education is integral to Newman's
opposition to the anti-dogmatic mind of his age. [60] For
by a general enlargement of mind, by a familiarity with
principles educed at various levels from matter—a familiarity which is acquired by allowing the mind to range at
large over the entire field of being—man is saved from
the cramping which pinches the positivist outlook on life.
It is not necessary to comment on the fact that Newman's
view here coincides with the practical policy, learned by
experience, which governs the view of the Church and
which has kept the ideal of a liberal education, *ceteris
paribus,* so much more alive among Catholics than among
others in the modern world. We find a source of melan-
choly in the fact that the pursuit of exact and accurate
knowledge through the mathematical and phyical sciences

45

wreaks havoc, *per accidens* but so regularly, in the indi
vidual mind. But we must face the facts. In this life ever
the pursuit of truth needs positive controls to be free o
vices.

NEWMAN AND HEGEL

Finally, the conclusion that the *Essay on Developmen*
is a particular manifestation of Newman's more radica
opposition to the anti-Christian elements of his age i
confirmed by a juxtaposition of the *Essay on Develop
ment* with the work of Hegel. A comparison between New
man and Hegel is too tempting an enterprise not to hav
been undertaken already, [61] and here we need only con
sider the comparison under one important aspect. Thi
will throw some light on the meaning of the fact that New
man's most significant break with his milieu occurred i
connection with a question of development.

No one was more intimately permeated with the ideal
istic temper of the world which Newman knew than Geor₁
Wilhelm Friedrich Hegel. Hegel found himself the cus
todian of substantially the same view of reality whicl
Newman encountered in his Protestant friends, the cus
todian of that Idea which had been the great depository
of European thought ever since Descartes. [62] Hegel fel₁
the movements of that Idea as it was brought into con
tact with the particular questions rising to the surface o₁
the intellectual ferment in the eighteenth- and nineteenth
century world. And, strangely enough, as he anxiously
watched the legacy he was guarding, the Idea bequeathed
to him by Descartes, Kant, and Schelling, at the very be
ginning of his career Hegel came to the conclusion that
the weakness of this Idea was precisely its want of a mech
anism of development. He says so explicitly in the first
pages of *The Phenomenology of Mind*, [63] and, true to
this prognosis set down in the book which was to be the
preface to his entire work, Hegel's whole philosophy of

esis, antithesis, and synthesis is an effort to remedy this efect.

Thus Hegel, who died fourteen years before the *Essay n Development* came into being, diagnoses as the weakess of the idealistic tradition the very point at which Jewman in the *Essay on Development* makes his decisive reak with the current of thought which he found prevaent in his world. We have Newman's exhaustive account f his own thought in the *Apologia,* as well as the thought self directly displayed in his voluminous works; and it s clear that he owes little if anything of his own impresions directly to Hegel. [64] The fact that nevertheless in the *Essay on Development* he finds and exploits in his enmy's lines the same weakness which had given Hegel so much concern confirms the conclusion that the *Essay on Development* is basically directed against the same elenental turns of thought which lay at the base of the idealstic tradition guarded by Hegel.

If at first sight this analysis seems discredited by the act that with the positivists, who were not idealists but naterialists, Newman's differences seem as radical as with he idealists themselves, the discrediting is only apparent; or at root the idealist and the materialist make the same rror. They try to reduce to simplicity what is not simple: world, and a corresponding mode of cognizing, which is adically bipolar. The idealist seeks to establish a simplicty by making everything Form, Mind, the Idea. The materialist seeks to establish simplicity by making everything Matter. In either event, the point at which human intellecion departs from the material (insofar as it can) is the rucial point; for it is the point at which the division underlying a dualistic world leaps most readily to the eye. Here the roads divide. The idealist goes his way saying hat there is nothing but Mind; the positivist goes his, insisting that there is plainly no Mind but only Matter. And t the same point of the departure of the intelligible from

47

the material, the realist—who earns his name primaril by facing facts—retains his self-possession and his humil ity under the stress of the intellectual concupiscence whic seeks the questionable satisfaction of simplification ever where simplification is impossible. He observes that i there are two basic components of the world, the bes thing to do is to admit it.

Newman in effect does just this. And in putting hi finger on the point where the intelligible emerges from the material, he finds the radical difference which divide both the idealist and the positivist from himself. If th idealist and the positivist are also opposed to one another the opposition is of relatively little moment. They are agreed on a basic point, which is that there is only one component of reality. This seems to be the only point o genuine concern to either; for the idealist and the materi alist or positivist grow up side by side, and they have al ways got along together pretty well.

CONCLUSION

Thus the *Essay on Development*, studied in its large historical and philosophical setting, reveals these genera facts. First, the book itself is for the most part a partic ular manifestation of Newman's radical opposition to the anti-Christian elements of his age, an opposition which is one facet of the whole Church's general opposition to the same elements. Secondly, Newman's stand in the *Es say on Development* is at root a demand for a view of reality which takes better account of the material com ponent in human intellection. In this sense, the *Essay on Development* shows how Newman's religious struggle with his age and his philosophical struggle with it are one and the same thing. For, although it is carried on in theologica territory, the dispute which the *Essay on Developmen* signalizes is conducted as a philosophical rather than as a theological dispute, as an attack on an error which is no primarily theological, [65] but which runs through any mon-

tic—idealistic or materialistic—explanation of reality, an
ror brought to bay by Newman at the point where the
telligible rises out of the material.

Viewing Newman's thought as a whole, we find three
mportant characteristics: (1) he persistently demanded
reconsideration of the nature of first principles; (2) he
iffered violently with the positivist tradition; and (3) he
roke most decisively with the intellectual tradition in
hich he had operated, over a question of development.
ll these facts reveal the same opposition which the analy-
s here proposed finds at the root of the argument of the
ssay on Development—an opposition to a faulty report-
ng of the origins of human intellection out of material
eing. First, quite as St. Thomas Aquinas had done before
im, Newman reduces the question of first principles di-
ectly to a question of the origin of the intelligible out of
aterial being. Secondly, his persistent opposition to the
ositivist-materialist mind manifests itself as a quarrel
ver first principles, and thus as a quarrel over the origin
f the intelligible out of the material. And thirdly, the
ery fact that the *Essay on Development* stands where it
oes in Newman's own intellectual odyssey—the very
act that at the point at which he parted definitively with
 whole mode of thought characteristic of his age, there
tands a dispute over the question of *development*—re-
eals again the same disagreement over the question of
he connection between the intelligible and the material.
or a dispute over the question of development had be-
ome highly significant in the nineteenth-century intel-
ectual world. No less a personage than Hegel had pointed
ut how awkward a business it was to have both the Idea [66]
anded down from Schelling and development at the same
ime. In defending the sort of development which he de-
ended Newman in effect came to blows with the idealis-
ic tradition. And the idealistic tradition is defined by its
eculiar notions concerning the intelligible and matter.
his last is the same quarrel over again.

In the present study, only the broad outlines of an interpretation have been attempted, with sufficient detail from Newman to substantiate the outline so far as it goes. This procedure has seemed justified prior to a handling of details, as a method of avoiding endless quibbles. Despite the eulogies of his clear style, Newman's thought, to one pursuing it closely, seems often to defy his powers of expression, so that it is difficult, if not at times impossible, to pull together everything that he says on any one subject into an absolutely satisfying whole. To examine the details of Newman's relation to Butler (an extremely important consideration) and the details of Newman's and Butler's analogies between the natural and the supernatural in connection with St. Thomas or with the "economies" of the Greek Fathers; to take up everything that Newman says about development and about first principles and to integrate it all with those things discussed here; to detail the relationship, here only roughly sketched, between Newman's thought and Hegel's—whether such studies may prove worth while is matter for further investigation.

NOTES

1 John Henry Cardinal Newman, *An Essay on the Development of Christian Doctrine* (16th impr.; London: Longmans, Green, and Co., 1920). This is the edition cited throughout the present article under the short title *Essay on Development*. First published in 1845, the book was republished in a revised form in 1878.

2 Newman's patristic studies furnish the matter for discussion through the entire book. In his Advertisement to the First Edition (*ibid.*, p. x), Newman apologizes for quoting so often from his own earlier works.

3 John Henry Newman, *Fifteen Sermons Preached before the University of Oxford between A.D. 1826 and 1843* (3d ed.; London, Rivingtons, 1872), pp. 312-51. For a discussion of this sermon, cf. James J. Byrne, "The Notion of Doctrinal Development in the Anglican Writings of J. H. Newman," *Ephemerides Theologicae Lovanienses*, XIV (1937), 230-86.

4 Wilfrid Ward, *The Life of John Henry Cardinal Newman* (New York: Longmans, Green, and Co., 1913), I, 4-5; cf. Newman's "Biglietto Speech" on the occasion of his elevation to the cardinalate, *ibid.*, II, 460. "The object of the [Oxford] Movement," Newman writes elsewhere, "was to withstand the Liberalism of the day" (*Apologia pro Vita Sua: The Two Versions of 1864 and 1865 Preceded by Newman's and Kingsley's Pamphlets* [London: Oxford University Press, 1913], p. 202; cf. also pp. 116-17, 164-74). In citing the last mentioned work here and elsewhere throughout the present study, the system of signs used to indicate differences between the 1864 and the 1865 text is disregarded as of no moment for the present purpose.

5 *An Essay in Aid of a Grammar of Assent* (London: Longmans, Green, and Co., 1901; first published in 1870) is an attempt to justify revealed religion epistemologically, as the *Essay on Development* is to justify it historically. The *Grammar of Assent* is the most important work of Newman's latter days. "How many times I have written it," he exclaims to Sister Imelda Poole (Ward, *Life*, II, 266; cf. II, 400, and II, 268, where Newman writes that he felt the *Grammar of Assent* would put a finish to his work).

6 Gordon Huntington Harper, *Cardinal Newman and William Froude, F. R. S.: A Correspondence* (Baltimore: The Johns Hopkins Press, 1933), p. 200.

7 *La philosophie de Newman: Essai sur l'idée de développement* (Paris: Boivin et Cie, 1933), p. XXXIX.

8 "St. Augustine and the Modern World," trans. by E. I. Watkin in *A Monument to Saint Augustine* by M. C. D'Arcy, S.J., Maurice Blondel, et al. (London: Sheed and Ward, 1930), p. 279. Cf. Erich Przywara, S.J., *J. H. Kardinal Newman*, in *Christentum: Ein Aufbau*, ed. by Otto Karrer, Bändchen IV, *Einführung in Newmans Wesen und Werk* (Freiburg i. Br.: Herder and Co., 1922), p. 13.

9 P. 175.

10 Ward, *op. cit.*, I. 60; cf. Newman, *Apologia*, p. 160.

11 Ward, *op. cit.*, I. 60; cf. 63-64.

12 Cf. Newman's letter of March 13, 1829, in Ward, *op. cit.*, I, 44-45.

13 John Henry Newman, *Letters and Correspondence of John Henry Newman during His Life in the English Church*, ed. by Anne Mozley (New York: Longmans, Green, and Co., 1911), II, 35, note 1. Cf. *Apologia*, p. 195.

14 *Apologia*, p. 107.

15 *Ibid.*, p. 117 ff.; Ward, *op. cit.*, I, 42.

16 *Apologia*, p. 136.

17 *Letters and Correspondence*, I, 18-22, 108-11; cf. *Apologia*, pp. 107-8. Newman's "conversion" recounted in these passages was not, however, of the approved Evangelical stamp, and after the publication of the *Apologia* Newman received well-intentioned letters from strangers or anonymous writers "assuring him that he did not yet know what conversion meant, and that the all-important change had still to be wrought in him if he was to be saved" (*Letters and Correspondence*, I, 108).

18 Newman cites an Anglican canon of the year 1603 to make this fact quite explicit (*Apologia*, p. 169; cf. *ibid.*, pp. 170 ff., 179).

19 *Apologia*, pp. 184-88.

20 *Ibid.*, pp. 179-82.

21 Cf. *ibid.*, p. 168, for Newman's earlier hopes to the contrary.

22 *Ibid.*, pp. 206, 236-41.

23 *Essay on Development*, p. 10 ff.; *Apologia*, p. 180 ff.

24 Cf. *The Via Media of the Anglican Church* (London: Longmans, Green, and Co., 1891), I, 201-9. But cf. also the adumbrations of the notion of development, *ibid.*, I, 53-54.

25 *Apologia*, p. 210 ff.

26 *Ibid.*, p. 211.

27 *Essay on Development*, pp. 122-34, 135-65.

28 *Ibid.*, p. 14.

29 *Ibid.*, pp. 35-36.

30 *Ibid.*, p. 41.

31 Newman groups these illustrations in certain quite serviceable but otherwise rather mongrel categories as political,

logical, historical, ethical, and metaphysical developments; cf. *Essay on Development*, pp. 42-54.

32 *Ibid.*, p. 43.

33 *Ibid.*, p. 148 ff.

34 *Ibid.*, pp. 37-38.

35 *Ibid.*, p. 35.

36 *Ibid.*, p. 34.

37 *Loc. cit.*

38 *Ibid.*, p. 36.

39 *Loc. cit.*

40 *Ibid.*, pp. 35, 34.

41 First published in 1736; the edition cited in the present study is *Bishop Butler's Analogy of Religion, Natural and Revealed, to the Constitution and Course of Nature*, with an analysis, left unfinished, by Robert Emory, D.D., ed. with a life of Bishop Butler by G. R. Crooks (New York: Harper and Brothers, 1894).

42 Cf. *Apologia*, p. 113. Newman himself was much more aware of Butler's influence on his thought and life than most commentators on Newman's works or students of his life have been. In speaking of the notions he got from Butler concerning sacramentalism (the analogy between and interrelation of the natural and the supernatural) and concerning probability as a guide of life, Newman calls these the "underlying principles of a great portion of my teaching" (*Apologia*, p. 113). And he seals the importance of Butler's influence by his self-composed epitaph, in which he sums up the whole of his life in terms of the first of these notions which he derived from Butler: *Ex umbris et imaginibus in veritatem* (Ward, *op. cit.*, II, 537) —that is, the natural world is only an analogous reflection of the full supernatural Truth. Moreover, Butler shows up at every stage of Newman's existence. In 1836, on the death of Hurrell Froude, his closest friend, Newman's first choice as a keepsake was Froude's volume of Butler's *Analogy* (*Apologia*, p. 173). Little wonder that Newman the Anglican should so choose; in a letter to Hawkins he styles Butler "the greatest name in the Anglican Church" (Guitton, *La philosophie de Newman*, p. XXII). The *Essay on Development* in 1845 not only quotes at great

length from the *Analogy,* but also uses many of Butler's examples as points of departure for discussion. Butler appears again in 1870 in the all-important *Grammar of Assent,* as well as in many other places in Newman's works. The though crystalized in Newman's famous statement that ten thousand difficulties do not make one single doubt (*Apologia,* p. 332) is Butler's (*Analogy,* pp. 307-8, and *passim*). Entries under Butler's name in Father Joseph Rickaby's *Index to the Works of John Henry Cardinal Newman* (London: Longmans, Green, and Co., 1914). p. 20, are significant so far as they go, but far from complete.

43 *Analogy,* pp. 86-88. Cf. the arguments throughout the book. Butler's argument at root was, of course, nothing new, nor had it been new even in the patristic age. It is foreshadowed in our Lord's words when Nicodemus balked at the notion of supernatural regeneration: do not be suprised that you fail to understand the supernatural workings of the Spirit (*spiritus,* pneuma); for you do not understand even the natural operations of the wind (*spiritus,* pneuma). "Non mireris quia dixi tibi: oportet vos nasci denuo. Spiritus ubi vult spirat: et vocem eius audis, sed nescis unde veniat, aut quo vadat: sic est omnis qui natus est ex spiritu. . . . Si terrena dixi vobis, et non creditis: quomodo, si dixero vobis caelestia, credetis?" (John 3:7-8, 12). A similar thought is expressed in the Old Testament passage which rides as an undercurrent through the conversation with Nicodemus: "Quomodo ignoras quae sit via spiritus, et qua ratione compingantur ossa in ventre praegnantis: sic nescis opera Dei, qui fabricator est omnium" (Eccles. 11:5).

44 Cf. e.g., Butler's remark that with regard to God's use of means for His ends "the mystery is as great in nature as in Christianity" (*Analogy,* p. 238, and *passim*).

45 Cf. the passage cited in the *Essay on Development,* p. 47.

46 *Ibid.,* p. 38.

47 *Essay on Development,* p. 56.

48 *Loc. cit.*

49 *Ibid.,* p. 57.

50 *Loc. cit.*

51 Cf., e.g., pp. 65, 68 ff., 186, 199.

52 *Essay on Development,* pp. 169-71.

53 Cf. *Essay on Development,* pp. 33-40, 55 ff.

54 For an his.orical discussion of this idealism, cf. Étienne Gilson, *The Unity of Philosophical Experience* (New York: Charles Scribner's Sons, 1937); and *id., Réalisme thomiste et critique de la connaissance* (Paris: Librairie Philosophique, J. Vrin, 1939).

55 Harper (ed.), *Cardinal Newman and William Froude, F. R.S.: A Correspondence,* p. 178.

56 *Ibid.,* p. 200. The bracketed material is supplied by Dr. Harper; Newman's letter never got beyond rough draft.

57 Cf. *Grammar of Assent,* pp. 422-23, 425-26. "Those who know nothing of the wounds of the soul, are not led to deal with the question, or to consider its circumstances; but when our attention is roused, then the more steadily we dwell upon it, the more probable does it seem that a revelation has been or will be given to us" (*Ibid.,* p. 423).

58 That is, from the knowledge "of our own extreme misery and need" (*Grammar of Assent,* p. 423; cf. pp. 423-25).

59 Cf. St. Thomas Aquinas, *Sum. Theol.* I, q. 1, a. 2 c.

60 Cf. *The Idea of a University* (London: Longmans, Green, and Co., 1902), pp. 124-25.

61 By Guitton, *op. cit.,* pp. 91-92, 141 ff., and *passim;* by Przywara in "St. Augustine and the Modern World," *A Monument to St. Augustine,* pp. 283-86.

62 Cf. Gilson, *The Unity of Philosophical Experience* and *Réalisme thomiste et critique de la connaissance.*

63 Of the Idea of Schelling and his school Hegel says: "The Idea, which by itself is no doubt the truth, really never gets any farther than just where it began, as long as the development of it consists in nothing else than such a repetition of the same formula" (*The Phenomenology of Mind,* trans. by J. B. Baillie [2d ed. rev.; London: George Allen and Unwin, Ltd., 1931], p. 78; cf. pp. 67-130).

64 Could Newman have derived from Hegel through Möhler, who is mentioned in the *Essay on Development,* p. 29? M. A. Minon in "L'Attitude de Jean-Adam Möhler (1796-1838) dans la question du développement du dogme," *Ephemerides Theologicae Lovanienses,* XVI (1939), 365,

points out that "Möhler voit en Hegel un panthéiste qui divinise l'esprit humain et ne laisse, par ailleurs, aucune place à l'immortalité personnelle. Toutefois, il n'y a pas que du mal chez Hegel. Möhler trouve que la conception hégélienne de l'histoire, de l'esprit absolu se matérialisant se réalisant et prenant peu à peu conscience de lui-même est une idée féconde." But the same author who discovers this relation between Möhler and Hegel discovers also that Newman does not find his inspiration in Möhler, whose notions on development are quite inferior to Newman's (*ibid.*, pp. 377-78). The same conclusion is reached by Henry Tristram in "J. A. Moehler et J. H. Newman: La pensée allemande et la renaissance catholique en Angleterre," *Revue des sciences philosophiques et théologiques* XXVII (1938), 184-204.

65 Cf. Byrne, "The Notion of Doctrinal Development in the Anglican Writings of J. H. Newman," *Ephemerides theologicae lovanienses,* XIV (1937), 285, where it is noted that Newman's "ideas" (of Christianity, etc.), at least in his Anglican writings, are not "objects of faith." The whole question of natural and supernatural is simply by-passed by Newman in the *Essay on Development;* see p. 35, where in effect, he enters his disclaimer.

66 Newman's persistent use of the term "idea" (in all sorts of senses) is to some extent, perhaps, Hegelian—the mark which the world he lived in and struggled against left on his mind.

Harold M. Petitpas

NEWMAN'S IDEA OF LITERATURE:
A HUMANIST'S SPECTRUM

Too many contemporary literary critics are so preoccupied with unearthing "literary fallacies" (whether they be of the personal or intentional or affective variety) that they ignore the manifest fallacy in their own restrictive approach to art and literature, discussing the works of art as though they were absolutely autonomous and hermitically sealed against the intrusions of the extra-aesthetic world. As an outgrowth of such a restrictive view, it is not surprising that much contemporary critical and creative work is so clinical and technical and ingenious in its emphasis, trying to cast upon literary studies an aura of scientific respectability. Nor is it surprising that the humanistic values inherent in great classical literature are so rarely alluded to in the contemporary criticism of literary works. According to this view, the greatness of an author like Shakespeare is to be accounted for not in terms of his comprehensive and complex personal vision of human experience, nor in terms of his halting but dexterous expression of such a vision, nor in terms of the aesthetic emotion that his work elicits, but exclusively in terms of ingenious worksmanship. To carry this contemporary approach to its logical conclusion, it would have to be said that a literary work does not speak to men; it speaks to itself. It exists in splendid isolation.

Reprinted by permission of RENASCENCE, XVII (1965).

In contrast to this contemporary trend of critical pur ism and monism, the critics of the eighteenth and nine teenth centuries, such as Addison, Johnson, Coleridge Arnold and Newman approached literary works with sensitive awareness of their humanistic values and impl cations. The critics of this older tradition would besto upon the literary artist the dignified role of public edu cator. Though the present study will be limited to New man's conception of literature, it should be remembere that his literary theory has affinities with such a classic critical tradition.

In reconstructing Newman's idea of literature, the tw principal sources to be used in this study will be his di courses on literature as they appear in *The Idea of a Un versity* and his essay on "Poetry with Reference to Ari totle's Poetics" as published in his *Essays Critical an Historical*. Supplementary evidence will be drawn from few of his other major works. [1] Newman's idea of lite ature will be revealed in terms of the four generally a cepted coordinates of art criticism: the artist, the wor the universe, and the audience.

In his idea of literature, Newman, with his characterist personalist approach to reality, focuses primary attentio on the literary artist. As opposed to the extreme forms contemporary de-personalism, he would have us rediscov er the person, the human presence, in artistic works. I the language of an author, Newman discovers the "faith ful expression of his intense personality, attending on h own inward world of thought as its very shadow; so th we might as well say that one man's shadow is another as that the style of a really gifted mind can belong to an but himself" (*The Idea*, p. 276). Pursuing this though further, he concludes that an author's language "express es not only his great thoughts, but his great self" (*Th Idea*, p. 280). In contrast to all mechanistic approaches t literature, he also insists that it is not "some productic

58

result attained by the partnership of several persons or machinery, or by any natural process, but in its very idea it proceeds, and must proceed, from some one given individual" (*The Idea,* p. 273). In opposition to a too technical approach to literature. Newman reprimands Aristotle for treating drama "more as an exhibition of ingenious workmanship than as a free and unfettered effusion of genius" (*ECH,* p. 7). In developing this thought, he adds that Aristotle entertained "too cold and formal conceptions of the nature of poetical composition as if its beauties were less subtle and delicate than they really are" (*ECH,* p. 8). In these passages, Newman is emphasizing that if a work makes us conscious of a distinct personal presence and of a distinct personal exercise of language, it has then passed a test of litmus-like accuracy to determine its literary genuineness.

In his approach to artistic vision, the Platonic cast of Newman's mind becomes readily apparent. For him, it is but natural to ask aloud why should not skill in diction be simply subservient, and instrumental to the great protoypal ideas which are the contemplation of a Plato or a Virgil?" (*The Idea,* p. 283). Furthermore, he would not allow the models by which great authors make their works become subordinate or irrelevant to art. In fact, in his view, it is the poet's supernal visions that color everything that his imagination engages: "It follows that the poetical mind is one full of the eternal forms of beauty and perfection; these are its material of thought, its instrument and medium of observation—these color each object to which it directs its view" (*ECH,* p. 10). It may be said that, for him, an artist without a vision is as a lover without a beloved.

Nor will Newman allow an author to become a mere linguistic dilettante. Rather he would have beautiful language be the fitting garb for beautiful thoughts. As he himself asks: Can we really think that "Homer, or Pindar, or Shakespeare, or Dryden, or Walter Scott were ac customed to aim at diction for its own sake, instead of being inspired with their subject and pouring forth beauti ful words because they had beautiful thoughts?" (*The Idea*, p. 279). That such a view is but an expression of Newman's habitual hierarchical approach to reality need no lengthy substantiation.

Moreover, Newman discovers the artist's presence with in a work not only through his vision and his thoughts but also through his diction, rhythm and imagery. For him, the diction and the rhythm pulsate harmoniously with the imagination and feelings that bodied them forth. As he explains about the artist, "not the words alone, but even the rhythm, the metre, the verse, will be the con temporaneous offspring of the emotion or imagination which possesses him" (*The Idea*, p. 279). To Newman meter is "but the outward development of the music and harmony within" (*ECH*, p. 10). Thus he would not ques tion the theory that contends that, whether he will it or not, a poet's meter tells tales about his inner soul. As to the image, Newman would regard it as "the sole outlet and expression of intense inward feeling" (*ECH*, p. 24). Imagery is thus not something ornamental, a mere accre tion, but it is rather the natural abode of revealing the author's feelings.

In thus stressing the personal quality of language and literature, Newman would have us re-focus our attention upon the dynamic origins of all artistic work—the artist himself. To rephrase another great English writer, he would have us see art as a personal signature.

The literary work itself—the focal point of much con temporary criticism—Newman views in terms of general and theoretical considerations. Such an approach may be explained by the fact that he was concerned with a gen eral theory of literature and not with the minute analysis of specific works. In the actual making of literary works e was particularly interested in the role of language. Because of his awareness of the inescapable limitations of language, he concedes that it is the "most pardonable fault of a poet" to fail in "clearness of style" (*G.A.*, p. 1). In other words, he sympathetically realized that in a literary work clarity in style might be but a reflection of a superficial mind and that obscurity in style might be but a reflection of a genuinely poetic mind. Futhermore, his recognition of the intrinsic limitations of language led him to stress the primary importance of metaphor in literary expression—in fact, in all human communication. For him, the poetic mind recognizes that "Figure is its necessary medium of communication with man; for in the feebleness of ordinary words to express its ideas, and in the absence of terms of abstract perfection, the adoption of metaphorical language is the only poor means allowed it for imparting to others its intense feelings" (*ECH*, p. 10). On the basis of this same view of language, Newman notes that Aristotle did not understand that "A word has power to convey a world of information to the imagination, and to act as a spell upon the feelings; there is no need of sustained fiction—often no room for it" (*ECH*, p. 8).

Also, in his reflections on language, he stresses the distinctive ways that the scientist, as contrasted to the literary artist, employs words. In his view, "science uses words merely as symbols, but literature uses language in its full compass, as including phraseology, idiom, style, composition, rhythm, eloquence and whatever other properties are included in it" (*The Idea*, p. 275). In the same context, developing this thought still further, he concludes that "Science, then, has to do with things, literature with thoughts."

In his observations on a classic's role in the formation and development of a language, Newman anticipates the views of such contemporary critics as T. S. Eliot. Thus, for him, the classic authors are really the "creators of

their language" (*The Idea*, p. 312). He says further, "T[
style of each of such eminent masters becomes henc[
forth in some sort a property of the language itsel[
words, phrases, collocations, and structure, which hithe[
to did not exist, gradually passing into the conversatio[
and the composition of the educated classes" (*The Ide[*
pp. 321-322). To him, the classics of a national literatu[
"have the foremost place in exemplifying the powers a[
conducting the development of its language" (*The Ide[*
p. 321). With Eliot, he would agree that the influen[
of a classic may undoubtedly act in such a way that [
may discourage anything new "rather than in that [
exciting rivalry or provoking reaction" (*The Idea*, p. 326[
With Eliot, he would also agree that a literary work do[
not exist in isolation—even if it be by nothing else tha[
its language, it exists within a tradition.

But it is particularly in his idea of poetry (in the com[
prehensive Aristotelian sense of that word) that Nev[
man's approach to the literary work is best revealed. Wi[
Aristotle he agrees that at least theoretically the exce[
lence of a tragedy depends upon its plot; but in viewi[
the Greek tragedy concretely and historically he disput[
this Aristotelian emphasis. As he says, "That the charm [
Greek tragedy does not ordinarily arise from scientif[
correctness of plot is certain as a matter of fact. Seldo[
does any great interest arise from the action; which, i[
stead of being progressive and sustained, is common[
either a mere necessary condition of the drama, or [
convenience for the introduction of matter more impo[
tant than itself" (*ECH*, p. 2). And, he concludes with th[
revealing comment: "It is not in the plot, but in th[
characters, sentiments and diction that the actual mer[
and poetry of the composition are found" (*ECH*, p. 2[
What Newman is really claiming is that Aristotle (th[
oretician that he was) discussed tragedy as it should [
rather than as it historically was. Though Newman w[
conscious of the hold of an imaginative work on the em[

ions, strangely he did not consider in his analysis the Aristotelian concept of catharsis.

In his observations on narrative as contrasted to dramatic literature, Newman reconsiders the relationship between plot and character in fiction. According to Newman, Scott in his Waverly novels is to be praised for exhibiting the necessary fictional interplay between plot and character. Byron, on the other hand, is to be censured for failing to exhibit such a "bearing of character and plot on each other" in his narrative poems (*ECH*, p. 19). In a remarkably penetrating criticism of Byron's narrative technique Newman censures the romantic poet for telling about his hero the Corsair instead of showing what the hero is (*ECH*, p. 19). He would not have the expository technique be confused with the narrative.

Since Newman places primary emphasis on the artist (as has already been indicated)—in his approach to the relationship between the work of art and the universe—he emphatically does not countenance the idea that the work of art offers but a mere copy of external reality. Rather agreeing with Aristotle, he regards poetry as a creation instead of a mere representation of experience. As he explains, poetry "supplies us with pictures drawn, not after an existing pattern, but after a creation of the mind. Fidelity is the primary merit of biography and history; the essence of poetry is fiction" (*ECH*, p. 9). And, reaffirming this same theory, Newman would have all artistic compositions adapt nature to human purposes: "Art is the development of nature, that is, its adaptation to the purposes of utility and beauty, the human intellect being the developing power" (*DCD*, p. 42). Applying this idealistic view of art to the novels of Miss Edgeworth, Newman criticizes her for justifying certain incidents in her novels on the grounds of their real life origin: "Such an excuse evinces a misconception of the principle of fiction which, being the perfection of the actual, prohibits the introduction of any such anomalies of experience (*ECH*, p. 14). It is not that Newman does not admit that the writer draws from life's experiences; rather it is that in art experience must be modified to conform to a creative idea.

Nor is art, for Newman, to be identified with natural history and philosophy. The poet, of course, may draw his subject matter from any aspect of reality. But, as a truly creative artist he transforms natural history and philosophy from a "bare collection of facts or principles" into an artistic work in which these facts and principles have a "meaning, beauty, and harmonious order not their own" (*ECH*, p. 12). Accordingly, depending from what perspective Plato be viewed, he may be regarded as a philosopher or a poet.

Nor is art, for Newman, to be identified with morality and religion. Weighing the different European literatures in the balance of his austere principles, he asserts that "One literature may be better than another, but bad will be the best, when weighed in the balance of truth and morality" (*The Idea*, p. 316). Developing this thought further, he sternly concludes that a national literature represents the "untutored movements of the reason, imagination, passions, and affections of the natural man, the leapings and the friskings, the plungings and the snortings, the sportings and the buffoonings, the clumsy play and the aimless toil, of the noble, lawless savage of God's intellectual creation" (*The Idea*, p. 317). And again, "On the whole, all Literatures are one; they are the voices of the natural man" (*The Idea*, p. 228). And finally, "Man's work will savour of man; in his elements and powers excellent and admirable, but prone to disorder and excess, to error and sin" (*The Idea*, p. 316). Because he sees man as being thus radically disordered, Newman cannot admit of even the possibility of a Christian literature. As he says, "If Literature is to be made a study of human nature, you cannot have a Christian Litrature. It is a contradiction in terms to attempt a sinless terature of a sinful man. You may gather something ery great and high, something higher than any Literature ever was; and when you have done so, you will find hat it is not Literature at all" (*The Idea,* p. 229). His ustere idealism and rigorous logic would seemingly permit him to entertain no other alternative.

It has been revealed what kind of relationships Newman discovers between the artistic work and the external osmos. It remains to be answered how he related the vork of art to its audience. First, let it be immediately mphasized that Newman recognized that the primary nd of art is pleasure and not instruction—a pleasure vhich to him must be the "refined and delicate enjoyment of the imagination" (*ECH,* p. 15). As his formal definition of poetry will confirm, he further related this aesthetic pleasure to the distinctive imaginative encounter vith beauty: "Poetry may be considered to be the gift of moving the affections through the imagination, and its bject to be the beautiful" (*ECH,* p. 29). He was also prepared to identify the distinct emotion that beauty elicited as being one of a tranquil feeling of admiration" *G.A.,* p. 109). Moreover, he insisted that the distinct poetical pleasure was not to be identified with that given by mere recognition: "If it be said, the fidelty of the imitation is often its greatest merit, we have only to reply, hat in such cases the pleasure is not poetical, but consists in the mere recognition" (*ECH,* p. 14). He was also aware that since images arise out of human experience hey can elicit a more vivid human response than can notions which arise out of abstraction (*G.A.,* p. 35). Finally, he was not blind to the fact that contact with what is beautiful and noble could have beneficial effects on an audience. Likewise, he realized that literature and art could lead men astray and could become an alluring substitute for the more austere demands of religion and morality.

In concluding this study of Newman's idea of literature the following three possible objections to his theory will be examined: 1) that he approaches the traditional critical problem of imitation in an overly idealistic manner; 2) that he misstates the problem of the relationship between literature and religion and morality; and 3) that inspired by a Puritan austerity he de-emphasizes the truly liberalizing effects of literary study.

The first possible objection that may be leveled against Newman's approach is that his view of the traditional critical category of "imitation" is Platonist rather than Aristotelian. It may be thus objected that rather than have the poet discover the Aristotelian ideal (the typical and universal as extracted from the individual and the particular), Newman would rather have him discover—in a kind of Shelleyan rapture—the supramundane Platonist ideal. And, as his own words confirm, "the poetical mind is one full of the eternal forms of beauty and perfection" (*ECH*, p. 10), he undoubtedly appears a legitimate target for such a criticism. But, on the other hand, interestingly enough, Newman was not oblivious to the fact that such a charge might be leveled against his theory. For, as he himself cautions, "Let it not be said that our doctrine is adverse to that individuality in the delineation of character which is a principal charm of fiction" (*ECH*, p. 15). Let us allow Newman himself to resolve this apparent tension between the "ideal" and the "real" in poetic composition: "It is not necessary for the ideality of a composition to avoid those minuter shades of differences between man and man, which give to poetry its plausibility and life; but merely such violation of general nature, such improbabilities, wanderings, or coarseness, as interfere with the refined and delicate enjoyment of imagination" (*ECH*, p. 15). And, developing this line of reasoning further, he will not admit that this theory excludes the treatment of evil in a literary composition. "The original conception of a weak or guilty mind may have its intrinic beauty; and much more so, when it is connected with a tale which finally adjusts whatever is reprehensible in the personages themselves" (*ECH*, p. 15). In short, Newman is insisting that in fiction it is the plot, the full narrative movement (what the work is trying to be) that reveals the literary artist's creative idea. It may be said that Newman's stress on the ideal encourages the development of fiction as an art form and not as a mere naturalistic copying of experience. Even though his approach may be thus defended, at least theoretically, the twentieth century critic, aware of Newman's idealistic and romantic bias, may still justifiably speculate as to whether the realistic tradition in fiction is reconcilable with his theory.

Perhaps the most serious criticism that can be advanced against Newman's idea of literature is that he misstated the nature of the relationship between literature and religion and morality. In order to spotlight the nature of the problem, it appears pertinent to restate his puzzling statement on the impossibility of a Christian literature: "If Literature is to be made a study of human nature, you cannot have a Christian Literature. It is a contradiction in terms to attempt a sinless literature of sinful man" (*The Idea*, p. 229). It may be asked whether Newman has not misconstrued the problem; whether he has not ignored the balance that he strove to establish between the "ideal" and the "real" in a literary composition? Whether he himself has not made a Christian literature impossible by requiring that its subject matter be a "sinless" one? As the following statement will reveal, his inability to conceive of Christian literature appears to be an outgrowth of how he believes evil is treated in a literary work; "If Physical Science be dangerous, as I have said, it is dangerous, because it necessarily ignores the idea of moral evil; but Literature is open to the more grievous imputation of recognizing and understanding it too well" (*The Idea*, p. 229). And, no doubt, his view was further reinforced by the recurring un-Christian (if

not anti-Christian) attitudes he discovered in such Euro
pean classic authors as Voltaire, Montaigne, Rabelai
Boccaccio and Ariosto. How rigorously he would app
his austere requirements for a Christian literature is ev
denced by his censure of even such a great Christian po
as Dante for his having placed in the Inferno a Pop
later to achieve ecclesiastical canonization (*The Idea,*
314 ff.). On the other hand, within Newman's ow
thought—as his praise of Shakespeare will testify—ther
may be found a much more liberal requirement that li
erature must satisfy to make it Christian. It may be wo
dered why Newman did not discover the essential pre
requisite of a Christian literature in the praise that h
bestowed on the English bard as upholding the "broa
laws of moral and divine truth" (*The Idea,* p. 318). Also
one might like to speculate as to why Newman did n
see a possibility of a Christian literature patterned afte
the spirit of such medieval writers as Langland or th
Pearl Poet, or after such seventeenth century poets a
Herbert, Crashaw, Vaughan, and Milton, or after suc
nineteenth century poets as de Vere, Thompson, Patmor
and Hawker. One might like to speculate further as t
how Newman might reconcile his conception of a Chris
tian literature with the work of such twentieth centur
writers as Claudel, Bernanos, Mauriac, Greene and Elio

As to the possible objection that Newman de-empha
sized the liberalizing effects of literary study, to refute
one has but to read his views on literature in *The Idea o
a University.* If he were truly hostile to the liberalizin
and cultural values of literary study, it would appear a
rather contradictory that he should argue so eloquentl
for the role of literature in a university education. If h
were thus so hostile, why would he regard classical civil
ization as being "so intimately associated with Christianit
that it may even be called the soil out of which Christi
anity grew" (*The Idea,* p. 262)? Why would he agre
with Clement and Origen that "Nature was a parable

68

Scripture was an allegory; pagan literature, philosophy, and mythology properly understood, were but a preparation for the Gospel" (*The Apologia, p. 24*)? From a purely secular point of view, Newman would be among the first to affirm that literary study has an inestimable value in equipping man to understand himself, his fellow men, and his milieu.

From this study of Newman's idea of literature, it has become readily apparent that his approach offers some sharp contrasts to certain trends in twentieth century criticism. As contrasted to those extreme realists who debate art by reducing it to but an uninspired reportorial account of human experience, he insists rather that art instead of merely copying reality uses experience for its own distinctive purposes after a pattern of the human mind. As contrasted to those extreme romantics who enthrone art as a quasi-religion, he assigns it its own distinctive perfection. As contrasted to those artistic purists who exalt language as an end in itself in literary activity, he recognizes that it must be made subservient to artistic vision. As contrasted to those depersonalists who mechanize literary activity, he emphasizes that a literary work is essentially a personal expression, man's defiant answer to machinocracy. And, as contrasted to those linguistic technicians who rigidly apply scientific analysis to literary works, he stresses that in genuine artistic expression there will always be a something that ultimately defies analytical explanation.

NOTE

All references in this study are to the standard editions of Newman's collected works published by Longman, Green, & Co., in 40 volumes, 1874-1921. Within the text, the following shortened references have been used: *The Idea of a University (The Idea); Essays Critical and Historical,* Volume I (*ECH*); *The Grammar of Assent, (G.A.); An Essay on the Development of Christian Doctrine, (DCD); The Apologia Pro Vita Sua (The Apologia).*

John Pick

NEWMAN THE POET

T. S. Eliot's "Gerontion" echoes Newman's "Dream of Gerontius." Yet the two poems epitomize the contrast between Newman's Gerontius, with his hard-won triumph of faith, and modern man with his "Thoughts of a dry brain in a dry season." "Lead, Kindly Light" continues to formulate for contemporary man "amid the encircling gloom" his unrest.

These two poems by Newman serve as a constant reminder of his many-sided genius. His *Apologia* remains possibly the greatest autobiography in English; his *Idea of a University* for a century has been recognized as the almost "perfect handling of a theory"; his *Development of Christian Doctrine* and *Grammar of Assent* are still relevant documents. In the forty volumes of his works we see him as preacher, orator, controversialist, novelist, theologian, and as poet, historian, philosopher, and critic.

But perhaps it is too much to expect that Newman be equally great in all these fields, and the question is often asked: Is he a poet?

It might be well to recall, with Eliot—the greatest religious poet of our own time—that "The capacity for writing poetry is rare; the capacity for religious emotion of

Reprinted by permission of RENASCENCE, VIII (1956).

the first intensity is rare; and it is to be expected that the existence of both capacities in the same individual should be rarer still."

It might be well also to recall that different people expect of poetry very different things. One remembers Dr Johnson's emphatic "If Pope be not a poet, where is poetry to be found?"—a different concept of poetry from that of Emily Dickinson who declared, "If I read a book and it makes my whole body so cold no fire can ever warm me I know that is poetry. If I feel physically as if the top of my head were taken off, I know that is poetry." She added: "These are the only ways I know it. Is there any other way?"

Readers have called Newman a poet, but they have meant various things. Opinions of his critics have varied all the way from one who contended that poetry was his ultimate gift to another who pronounced: "It is not poetry at all—not even the protoplasm of poetry." But even this latter critic—J. Lewis May—has queried and then answered:

Was, then, Newman a poet? To this question there is but one answer. A poet he certainly was. But he was a poet who did not write poetry. His real poetry is to be found, not in his metrical composition, which affect one with a sense of chill disappointment, but in his prose.

All students of Newman, even the most critical, have found poetry—and great poetry—in his sermons, and of all the Victorian preachers (and it was an age of great pulpit orators such as Canon Liddon, Dean R. W. Church Frederick D. Maurice, Dean Stanley, Charles Kingsley and Thomas Arnold) probably only Newman's sermons are still read.

Even without the physical presence of Newman before one, Matthew Arnold's passage on his sermons conveys their poetry:

Forty years ago, when I was an undergraduate at Oxford, voices were in the air there which haunt my memory still. . . . Who could resist the charm of that spiritual apparition, gliding in the dim afternoon light through the aisles of St. Mary's, rising into the pulpit, and then, in the most entrancing of voices, breaking the silence with words and thoughts which were a religious music,—subtle, sweet and mournful? I seem to hear him still, saying: "After the fever of life, after weariness and sickness, fightings and despondings, langour and fretfulness, struggling and succeeding; after all the changes and chances of this troubled, unhealthy state,—at length comes death, at length the beatific vision." . . . Again I seem to hear him: "The season is chill and dark, and the breath of the morning is damp, and worshippers few, but all this befits those who are by their profession penitents and mourners, watchers and pilgrims. More dear to them that loneliness, more cheerful that severity, and more bright that gloom, than all those aids and appliances of luxury by which men nowadays attempt to make prayer less disagreeable to them. True faith does not covet comforts; they who realize that awful day, when they shall see Him face to face whose eyes are as a flame of fire, will as little bargain to pray pleasantly now as they will think of doing so then."

In these quotations the reader catches the magic of Newman's voice, the passion of his words—the poetry of Newman. The sermons with their impassioned cadences and rhythms, their imaginative power, their sudden illumination of the abstract by the use of the concrete, their analogies and metaphors—one who reads them cannot help saying: here is a poet in the pulpit.

But even such austerely intellectual works as *The Development of Christian Doctrine*, the *Idea of a University* or *The Grammar of Assent* are not without their poetry which resides not only in their panoply of cadence, alliteration and climax, but even in such individual words as one of his commentators has pointed out: "A University is the place where the catechist *makes good his ground* as he goes, *treading in* the truth day by day into his ready memory, and *wedging* and *tightening* it into the expanding reason."

But if all readers have detected the poetry of his prose, not all of them have felt the poetry of his verse. However, two of Newman's poems have become classics, and strangely enough one was written at almost the opening of his poetic career and the other at the close.

"Lead, Kindly Light" is so famous—it is said that more than forty musical settings have been written for it—that analysis need not detain us here, though the intensity and architectonic structure of this *de profundis* ought to be noted.

It is a short poem, only three stanzas long, while "The Dream of Gerontius," the other poem that is popularly linked with Newman's name, is the longest he ever attempted—almost a thousand lines. Acclaimed during Newman's life, it has retained much of its popularity. In his own day even Swinburne praised it; General Gordon kept it with him at Khartoum as he awaited his death. It had been translated into French and German. During the first two decades after Newman's death over eighty thousand copies were sold.

In 1865 Newman composed it under the presentiment —he was then sixty-five but was to live to be ninety—that he was to die and in three short weeks, with scarcely a correction, he completed the poem. The story is told that some weeks later the editor of *The Month* asked him for a theological contribution and that Newman, after hunting through his desk to see whether he had anything suitable on hand, came across "The Dream of Gerontius" and forwarded it to the editor saying that he was sorry he had nothing else completed.

The theme of "The Dream of Gerontius," that of the Christian facing death and of the disappearance of the veil between this and the next life, had been foreshadowed and anticipated in many of his minor poems and sermons, and one writer has aptly remarked that all of his previous works are "an overture to the grand Requiem."

74

in spite of shortcomings, the poem has been highly regarded, even by those not in sympathy with Newman, for its psychological penetration, its presentation of the mind of a dying man."

Just as impressive is the skillful versification. The poem depends not upon the eye (there is little of the visual power of a Dante) but upon the ear. It is not surprising that such a man as Elgar has elaborated its music and that hymns have been made of separate stanzas. In 1951 it was performed in London as a dramatic poem with new music by Fernand Laloux.

The prosody bends and flexes to the meaning with supple and subtle ease, and the poem is filled with astonishing contrasts and variety. The rhythm is at times stately, or pleasing, or despairing, or hopeful, or awesome and solemn or anguished or calm. The contrast, for instance, between the graceful harmonies of the angelic choirs and the cacophanous dissonances of the demons is masterful. Especially notable is the lyrical close "Farewell, but not for ever!"

Part of the impressiveness of the poem is due to the degree to which Newman has deftly woven into the poem his own translation of liturgical chants, and litanies, and psalms from the Bible.

"The Dream of Gerontius" is an answer to his own earlier "Lead, Kindly Light." It is also an expansion of his own epitaph, *Ex umbris et imaginibus in veritatem*— out of shadows and insubstantialities into realities.

But both "Lead, Kindly Light" and "The Dream of Gerontius" have been widely anthologized and are well known. What of Newman's other poetry? It is uneven in quality—this is notoriously true, of course, even of such men as Wordsworth—and Newman, who took a very modest view of his own poetry, anticipated the need for selection. In the preface to his collected poems, entitled simply and unpretentiously *Verses on Various Occasions*, he remarked humbly that only the urging of others had brought him to the project and that "biassed by the associations of memory and by general feelings," and faced with the choice of either printing all or none, he chose the former course.

The virtues of the best poems are found in the sureness with which he handles verse forms, in their lucidity, and above all in the highly personal quality of the sincerity candor, and humility of the spiritual struggle of a burdened and troubled soul. Dignity and restraint sometimes raise them to a severe beauty.

The reader easily discovers the strength of Newman's best poems, but he also discovers—even in "The Dream of Gerontius"—numerous weaknesses. In his lesser poems he will often be deeply disappointed. What are the defects and limitations? Playing *advocatus diaboli,* one of his recent critics, Charles Frederick Harrold, indicted Newman along with the group to which he belonged:

It is one of the ironies of the Oxford Movement that it poetry should have been so feeble. Unfortunately, Tractarian poets seem to have felt that graceful versifying of approved sentiments, ornamented with metaphor and some eighteenth-century "poetic diction," was a satisfactory method of writing religious poetry.

Much of Newman's inferior verse is not "simple, sensuous and passionate." The restraint is too great and there is a lack of lyric ardor, of creative imaginative power and intensity. Only rarely is there pictorial power, or sharply focused imagery. What Newman himself referred to as "vivid exactness" is absent.

Conventional poetic diction and clichés (festive-hall, dewy morn and balmy eve, pensive brow, azure heaven, golden flowers, dazzling beams, starry height, fair domain, sweet music, earth's green robes, vaulted sky) and poetic archaisms are not unusual and are sometimes found even in his better poems. Corresponding to the absence of

vivid exactness" there is also a tendency toward gener-
ization and the personification of abstractions (Death,
leasure, Affection, Zeal, Fear, Charity, Time, Anger,
y, Sin, Truth). Metaphors are rarely bold or striking,
e language seldom compressed, and there is an absence
f "word magic," of hidden music, of subtle rhythms. Ob-
ous rhymes abound.

At its worst it becomes pedestrian and prosily wooden:

> Plants in the garden
> See best the Sun's glory;
> They miss the green sward in
> A conservatory.

nd very characteristic is the tendency to preach, to be
idactic and philosophically moralistic; not unusual is the
nal stanza of "St. Paul at Melita":

> But, when he felt the viper's smart,
> Then instant aid was given;
> Christian! hence learn to do thy part,
> And leave the rest to Heaven.

luch of his verse, then, may be said to belong to "the
terature of knowledge" rather than to "the literature of
ower."

If these are frequent defects of Newman's poetry then
ne can ask whether there are any particular ways of ac-
ounting for them, and I think that it is quite possible to
ome close to a series of interrelated answers.

Newman's critical sense was keen in reference to his
wn prose but it was weak when he came to his own
oetry. Indeed his criticism of poetry, particularly during
is early career, is notoriously mixed. He thought of Pope
s "a rival of Shakespeare, in copiousness and variety if
ot in genius." Of his immediate predecessors he knew
ttle of Wordsworth and Byron, almost nothing of Cole-
idge, Shelley or Keats. His greatest favorite was Scott

77

and after him came Crabbe and Southey. In a letter Gerar Manley Hopkins remarked that Newman's preference fo the opening of Southey's *Thalaba* over the first chorus Milton's *Samson Agonistes* "is as if you were to compa the Panathenaic frieze and a teaboard and decide in th teaboard's favor." Newman's critical sense was inde sometimes strange.

This may partially be accounted for by the fact th Newman's only really productive period of writing poeti came at a peculiar time, the 1830's. It was a season whe the Romantics had passed their zenith—by 1830 most them had died—and at a time when the luminaries of th Victorian era, Browning and Tennyson, had not as y established themselves, a period which one of the literar historians has aptly called "the interregnum," when thos poets who had long been in the ascendancy had been swep away and their places remained unfilled. It was therefor an era of poetic mediocrity and uncertainty. During th period Newman's poetic taste was formed.

It is crucial to a right understanding of the limitation of Newman's poetry to be aware of the stage of develop ment in his life during which he wrote most of it. New man's life stretches across most of the nineteenth century from 1801 to 1890, but his most poetic period started i 1828; then during his Mediterranean tour of 1832-1833 immediately preceding the initiation of the Oxford Move ment in 1833, he wrote half of the poetry he was ever t write.

In 1836 he published (with other poets of the Oxfor Movement) *Lyra Apostolica* which included most of hi poems up to that date. In 1845 he became a Roman Cath olic and between that date and 1865 when he wrote hi greatest poem, "The Dream of Gerontius," he produce little poetry, and much of that was mere translation. Th final volume of his poetry, what might be called his col lected works, appeared in 1868 and was entitled *Verse on Various Occasions*. More than half had already appeared in *Lyra Apostolica*.

Since his most productive period was from 1828 to 1833 and since it was during this period that his practice of writing was set, a valuable way of trying to account for the limitations of his poetry is to discover what his critical and aesthetic position was during that period.

In 1828 Newman wrote a critical essay of over ten thousand words (published in 1829) entitled *Poetry with Reference to Aristotle's Poetics*, an essay which is by no means strictly Aristotelian—nor even consistent within itself—and which dominated him during the years of his greatest productivity and for many years after.

Moving away from the rationalism of the Oriel Noetics and from the influence of Whately (on whose *Logic* he had worked), now fearful of the "usurpations of reason," he holds a rather romantic theory of inspiration according to which poetry is "a free and unfettered effusion of genius." That such a view was no passing fancy is reflected in a letter to a friend in 1833 in which he says, "Ten thousand obvious ideas become impressive when put into metrical shape; and many of them one should not dare to utter except metrically," and he adds very significantly, "for thus the responsibility (as it were) is shoved off of oneself."

The theory of poetry as "a free and unfettered effusion of genius" meant that he looked at his poetry in a very different way from his prose. Poetry became a mere "spontaneous overflow of powerful feelings" while prose was disciplined to perfection. That this was his view is further substantiated by the fact that it is notorious that he found poetry easy and seldom worked over it while he spent endless hours on his prose. It was of his prose that he wrote: "Every book I have written has been a sort of operation, the distress is so great." Of one of his theological volumes he said to his sister:

I write, I write again; I write a third time in the course of six months. I literally fill the paper with corrections, so that another person could not read it. I then write it out fair for the printer. I put it by; I take it up; I begin to correct again; it will not do. Alterations multiply; pages are rewritten, little lines sneak in and crawl about. The whole page is disfigured; I write again; I cannot count how many times this process is repeated.

On the other hand, during his Mediterranean tour he sometimes "was inspired" to dash off two or three poems in a single day and we never hear of him correcting or revising them. His poetry, according to his accounts (and unfavorable critics will say it is easy to detect this), seems to have written itself.

In his *Poetry with Reference to Aristotle's Poetics* he also holds a moralistically didactic view which is very evident in the poetry he wrote during this period. It was part of his reaction at this time against liberalism; one recalls the passage in the *Apologia* in which he says: "The truth is, I was beginning to prefer intellectual excellence to moral, I was drifting in the direction of the Liberalism of the day." He bent over backwards to over-emphasize the moral element in poetry. In his essay on poetry he goes so far as to say, "Without affecting the accuracy of a definition, one might call [poetic talent] the originality of right moral feeling" and "poetry is ultimately founded on correct moral perception," "a right moral state of heart is the formal and scientific condition of a poetical mind." Poetry must "satisfy the moral nature." It is significant that it was because he felt that they inculcate moral virtue that he especially approved of Crabbe and Southey. Poetry becomes a moral teacher and "right moral feeling" becomes the criterion of poetry. Such quotations can be multiplied from the Newman of this period (for Newman's views changed later), but the following is particularly conclusive:

With Christians, a poetical view of things is a duty,—we are bid to colour all things with hues of faith, to see a Divin meaning in every event, and a superhuman tendency. . . . It may be added, that the virtues peculiarly Christian are especially poetical—meekness, gentleness, compassion, contentment, modesty, not to mention the devotional virtues; whereas the ruder and more ordinary feelings are the instruments of rhetoric more justly than of poetry—anger, indignation, emulation, martial spirit and love of independence.

Such views were reinforced by the Evangelistic upbringing which overemphasized a view which was, in the words of one critic, "morally severe and non-aesthetic."

Accompanying such opinions in his essay on poetry was another view which would make impossible a poetry that would be "simple, sensuous and passionate." Holding that poetry "becomes, moreover, the utterance of right moral feeing, seeking a purity and truth which the world will not give," he Platonically rejected the world of the senses, saying that "the poetical mind is full of eternal forms of beauty and perfection," in contrast to "the commonplace and matter-of-fact conceptions of ordinary minds, which are fettered down to the particular and individual." His suspicion of the concrete and particular at this time appears not in his prose for his letters are often delightfully vivid descriptions, and his friend Thomas Mozley wrote:

His eye quickly caught any sudden glory or radiance above; very prismatic hue or silver lining; every rift, every patch of blue. . . . His admiration of the beauties of earth and sky, his quickness to observe changes overhead, and the meaning he put into them, sometimes taxed the patience of a dull observer. Flowers, especially certain flowers, he was fond of as a child could be.

But this hardly evidences itself in his poetry; instead he wrote such lines as these from "The Pilgrim" (1831):

There stray'd awhile, amid the woods of Dart,
    One who could love them, but who durst not love.
A vow had bound him, ne'er to give his heart
    To streamlet bright, or soft secluded grove.
'Twas a hard humbling task, onwards to move

> His easy-captured eyes from each fair spot,
>   With unattach'd and lonely step to rove
> O'er happy meads, which soon its print forgot:—
> Yet kept he safe his pledge, prizing his pilgrim-lot.

Or such verses as these from "The Isles of the Sirens" (1832):

> Cease, Stranger, cease those piercing notes,
>   The craft of Siren choirs;
> Hush the seductive voice, that floats
>   Upon the languid wires.
>
> Music's ethereal fire was given
>   Not to dissolve our clay,
> But draws Promethean beams from Heaven,
>   And purge the dross away.
>
> Weak self! with thee the mischief lies,
>   Those throbs a tale disclose;
> Nor age nor trial has made wise
>   The Man of many woes.

In contrast are such lines as the following from "To Edward Caswall":

> Once, o'er a clear calm pool,
> The fulness of an over-brimming spring,
> I saw the hawthorn and the chestnut fling
> Their willing arms, of vernal blossoms full
> And light green leaves: the lilac too was there,
> The prodigal laburnum, dropping gold.

But these lines belong to 1858, a different period of Newman's development.

His mature views of poetry belong to the time when he had almost ceased to write poetry and they may be found especially in *The Idea of a University* and in addresses at that period such as "Christianity and Letters" and "Catholic Literature in the English Tongue."

A narrowly didactic and moralistic view disappears. ot only does he hold that the greater writer subjects his ork to severe correction, but he says in *Idea of a University*:

> Literature does not argue, but declaims and insinuates; it multiform and versatile: it persuades instead of convincing, seduces, it carries captive; it appeals to the sense of honour, to the imagination, or to the stimulus of curiosity; it makes its way by means of gaiety, satire, romance, the beautiful, the leasurable.

nd every reader of *The Grammar of Assent* knows that y 1870 so far has he reacted against Platonism that it is ow not the "notional" but "the real" which seems to him fair.

Newman's mature views could have resulted in a very ifferent kind of poetry than that which we now associate ith his name, but his poetically productive period was ver and his views mellowed slowly. His aesthetic was ow more solid, but his creative spirit went into his great rose.

What, then, is the value of much of Newman's poetry? argely, I think, in the contribution of his productive eriod of poetry to the formation of one of England's reatest prose styles. Often the things which are defects poetry became virtues in prose; if, for instance, poems nould not preach, then certainly sermons should, and Jewman brought to his prose as the years went on many oetic qualities so subtly controlled and so deftly woven ito the fabric of his work that the final outcome was a tyle which without being "poetic prose" yet has the modlations, the cadences, the metaphorical overtones that ive to his prose an important part of its continuing appeal.

Frank O'Malley

THE THINKER IN THE CHURCH:
THE SPIRIT OF NEWMAN

ecent reports reach us from England that a notable ele-
ent in support of the cause of Cardinal Newman's can-
ization is the unusual extent of American devotion to
m and to his thought. Certainly the name of Newman
great among us. Most American Catholic thinkers
ould agree with Otto Karrer, writing in April, 1947, for
he Review of Politics on Newman and the spiritual
isis of the Occident, that Newman is probably "the most
ustrious religious mind in the modern Anglo-Saxon
orld." It is clear that he is the truly great eminence at
e start of the Catholic intellectual renascence of the past
ndred years. In our devotion to him and in our praise
him as a foremost thinker in the Church, it is well to
nsider what is the justification for the esteem in which
e hold him.

What was the spirit of this man who is with us a con-
ant reference and a standard and a sign? We need to
etermine it carefully because even in the moment of
sing his name and imprinting it upon a cause or action
point-of-view, we may not actually understand the be-
g who bore the name, we may not realize the true qual-
es of the mind and heart of the man we revere and ac-

eprinted by permission of THE REVIEW OF POLITICS, XXI,
o. 1 (January 1959).

claim. Not really understanding him, we can and do re___ ily take his name in vain, abuse the name of one of ___ greatest modern Englishmen, attach it to enterprises a___ activities he would surely have abhorred. So we misr___ resent Newman. We cry up his name—and do not rea___ care what he said or what he meant or what he was ___ long as we can comfort ourselves under the splendor ___ his distinction. Thus, while blessing ourselves with hi___ we are only confusing ourselves and others—and har___ honoring the human being whose greatness becomes ___ stereotype, a monumental but hollow word. What, th___ was the quality of Newman? What was the real won___ of his humanity, of his spirit as a thinker in the Churc___ as a man, a teacher, and a prophet? Using Newman's o___ words as much as possible, we shall try, if not fully ___ least implicitly, suggestively and quite personally, to ___ swer the question.

I

We can say first that his spirit was liturgical, that ___ the spirit of Newman moved within the spirit of the lit___ gy, the liturgy thought of in its most significant sense ___ the very rhythm of Christian existence, stirred and c___ tered by the life of Christ. Newman absorbed the liturgi___ character of existence. He lived by the liturgy; specifica___ applying the words of Romano Guardini, himself a Ne___ man type of thinker in the twentieth century, he was "___ by the rule and love of the Holy Ghost to a life in Chr___ and in Him for the Father." The liturgy is not, as so___ say, aestheticism. It is real. It demands self-subjection, ___ disciplining of the inner life, never the flagrant and c___ otic cultivation of the ego in the arbitrary and capricio___ The liturgy is reality, physical and metaphysical. Neit___ thought nor emotion, it is "a process of fulfillment, ___ growth to maturity." It involves not the selfish unive___ of the individual but all creation: "Under Christ ___ Head, the Church gathers together 'all which is in Heav___

Earth, and under the Earth'." Guardini explains, in *The Church and the Catholic and the Spirit of Liturgy*, that in the act of worship directed towards God, everything is linked and "as a whole embraced in the relation with God established by prayer; the fullness of Nature, looked and transfigured by the fullness of grace, organized by the organic law of the Triune God, and steadily flowing according to a rhythm perfectly simply yet infinitely rich; the vessel and expression of the life of Christ and the Christian—this is the liturgy. The liturgy is crean redeemed and at prayer because it is the Church at prayer." This sense of Christ-in-time, of Christ-in-the-universe, of every age flowing and of every man growing His Great Body—this Incarnational view—Newman held profoundly and it affected and controlled his attitude towards time and man and the problems of time and human society.

These are some very few of the words of Newman, expressing the spirit of the liturgy: Christ, he says, "left His Father's courts, He was manifested, He spake; and His voice went out into all lands. He has taken to Himself His great power and reigned; and, whereas an enemy is the god and tyrant of this world, as Adam made it, so, as far as He occupies it, does He restore it to His Father. Henceforth He is the one principle of life in all His servants who are but His organs. The Jewish church looked towards Him; the Christian speaks and acts from Him. What is prior to Him is dark, but all that comes after Him is illuminated. The Church, before His manifestation offered Him material elements 'which perish with the using'; but now He has sent His spirit to fill such elements with Himself, and to make them living and availing sacrifices to the Father. Figures have become means of Grace, shadows are substances, types are Sacraments in Him. What before were decent ordinances and pious observances, have now not only a meaning but a virtue. Water could but wash the Body in the way of Nature; but now it acts toward the cleansing of the soul. 'Wine which ma[k]eth glad the heart of man' and 'bread which strengthe[ns] man's heart' nay, the 'oil which maketh him a cheerf[ul] countenance' henceforth are more than means of anim[al] life, and savour of Him. Hands raised in blessing, t[he] accents of the voice of man, which before could not sy[m]bolize the yearnings of human nature, or avail for low[er] benefits, have now become the 'unutterable intercessio[n]' of the Spirit, and the touch, and the breath of the Inca[r]nate Son. The Church has become His Body, her pries[ts] His delegates, her people His members." This, Newma[n] appends, is what Christ has done by His coming.

In another passage he declares: "Christ Himself vouc[h]safes to repeat in each of us in figures and mystery [all] that He did and suffered in the flesh. He is formed [in] us; born in us, suffers in us, rises again in us, lives in [us,] and this not by succession of events, but all at once; f[or] He comes to us as a spirit, all dying, all rising again, [all] living. We are ever receiving our birth, our justificatio[n,] our renewal, ever dying to sin, ever rising to righteousne[ss.] His whole economy in all its parts is ever in us all [at] once; and this divine presence constitutes the title of ea[ch] one of us to heaven; this is what He will acknowled[ge] Himself, and His image in us, as though we reflect[ed] Him, and He, on looking roundabout, discerned at on[ce] who were His; those, namely, who gave back to Him H[is] image."

Newman also notes that, while Socrates wished to i[m]prove man, "he laid no stress on their acting in concert [in] order to secure that improvement; on the contrary, t[he] Christian law is political, as certainly as it is moral. W[hy] is this? It arises out of the intimate relation between H[im] and His subjects, which, in bringing them all to Him [as] their common Father, necessarily brings them to ea[ch] other. Our Lord says, 'Where two or more are gather[ed] together in My Name, I am in the midst of them.' Fello[w] ship between His followers is made a distinct object and duty, because it is a means, according to the provisions of His system, by which in some special way they are brought near to Him. . . . The almighty King of Israel was ever, indeed, invisibly present in the glory above the ark, but he did not manifest Himself there or anywhere else as a present cause of spiritual strength to His people; but the new King is not only ever present, but to every one of His subjects individually is He a first element and perennial source of life. He is not only the Head of His kingdom, but also its animating principle and its centre of power."

Finally, we must cite Newman's famous description of the marvelous Action of the Mass, the central act of worship in the Church: "The Mass is not a mere form of words,—it is a great action, the greatest action that can be on earth. It is not the invocation merely, but if I dare use the word, the evocation of the Eternal. He becomes present on the altar in flesh and blood, before whom Angels bow and devils tremble . . . words are necessary, but as means, not as ends; they are not mere addresses to the throne of grace, they are instruments of what is far higher, of consecration, of sacrifice. . . . Each in his own place, with his own heart, with his own wants, with his own thoughts, his own intention, with his own prayers, separate but concordant, watching what is going on, watching its progress, uniting in its consummation;—not painfully and hopelessly following a hard form of prayer from beginning to end, but, like a concert of musical instruments, each different but concurring in a sweet harmony, we take our part with God's priest, supporting him, yet guided by him."

II

Because Newman's spirit was liturgical—here it has been recorded—it could not have been rationalistic, that is, Newman's vision could not have stopped with the lim-

its of logic, with the walls of the world. The doctrine of
the Incarnation, he observes, must be regarded as "the
announcement of a divine gift conveyed in a material and
visible medium, it being thus that heaven and earth are
in the Incarnation united." The universe to Newman, because of his consciousness of the Incarnation, was unfinished. Christ had entered into it and it could never be
closed again. The supernatural had touched the natural
and the mind of man could not—tidily and categorically
—shape it and control it as if it were utterly of itself and
by itself. The narrow eye of a narrow reason could see
the universe as finished, as perfectly and neatly manage-
able. But the wide, inseeing eye of Newman could see it
as wide-open to the "effluences of His grace." Yet the
civilization in which he lived was essentially rationalistic,
just as ours is, narrow, superficial and arbitrary, moving
along the surfaces, descending into the depths of the
spiritual underworld only in its rarest men, like Blake,
Hopkins, Kierkegaard, Dostoievski, Soloviev (once termed
a Russian Newman), Bloy, and Newman himself—these
of course, bringing to mind the older Pascal and the an-
cient Augustine. Newman especially, living in the spirit
of the liturgy, could not have abided the rationalistic temper of the time. But, note well, that *it was not against
reason* that Newman inveighed, only against its usurpations and abuses, the narrowing of the range of human
vision into technical formulas, the confinements of logical propositions and the complacencies of analysis. It is
no credit, Newman says, for any man to deal with only
what he considers rational. There is much beyond. "No
analysis," he remarks, "is subtle and delicate enough to
represent adequately the state of the mind under which
we believe, or the subjects of belief, as they are presented
to our thoughts." Of logical analysis, he says again, that it
is but an account of the progress of reasoning: "it does
not make the conclusion correct; it does not make the in-
ference rational. . . . It does but give [a man] a sustained

90

consciousness, for good or for evil, that he is reasoning. How a man reasons is as much a mystery as how he remembers." He further says, "While we talk logic, we are unanswerable; but then on the other hand, this universal living scene of things is after all as little a logical world as it is a poetical. . . ."

Newman describes the action of rationalism: ". . . it is rationalism to accept the Revelation, and then to explain it away; to speak of it as the word of God, and to treat it as the word of man; to refuse to let it speak for itself; to claim to be told the *why* and *how* of God's dealings with us, as therein described, and to assign to Him a motive and scope of our own; to stumble at the partial knowledge which He may give us of them; to put aside what is obscure, as if it had not been said at all; to accept one-half of what has been told us, and not the other half; to assume that the contents of Revelation are also its proof; to frame some gratuitous hypothesis about them, and then to garnish, gloss and color them, to trim, clip, pare away, and twist them, in order to bring them into conformity with the idea to which we have subjected them." And Newman suggests what happens when we are content to look at the history of man through a rationalistic focus: "Christianity will melt away in our hands like snow; we shall be unbelievers before we at all suspect where we are. With a sigh we shall suddenly detect the real state of the case. We shall look on Christianity, not as a religion, but as a past event which exerted a great influence on the course of the world, when it happened, and gave a tone and direction to religion, government, philosophy, literature, manners; an idea which developed itself in various directions strongly, which was, indeed, from the first materialized into a system—a church, and is still upheld as such by numbers, but by an error; a great boon to the world, bestowed by the Giver of all good, as the discovery of printing may be, or the steam engine, but as incapable of continuity, except in its effects, as the shock of an earthquake, or the impulsive force which commenced the motions of the planets."

Newman compares the intellectual greatness of the philosophers of the world with the greatness seen in Christ and His Saints: "We know that philosophers of this world are men of deep reflection and inventive genius, who propose a doctrine and by its speciousness gather round them followers, found schools, and in the event, do wonderful things. These are the men, who at length change the face of society, reverse laws and opinions, subvert governments, and overthrow kingdoms; or they extend the range of our knowledge, and, as it were, introduce us into new worlds. Well, this is admirable, surely, so vast is the power of the mind; but, observe how inferior is this display of intellectual greatness compared with that which is seen in Christ and His Saints, inferior because defective. These great philosophers of the world, whose words are often so good and so effective, are themselves too often nothing more than words. Who shall warrant for their doing as well as speaking? They are shadows of Christ's prophetical office, but where is the sacerdotal or the regal? Where shall we find in them the nobleness of the King, and the self-denial of the priest? On the contrary, for nobleness they are often 'the meanest of mankind'; and for self-denial the most selfish and cowardly. They can sit at ease and follow their own pleasure and indulge the flesh, or serve the world, while their reason is so enlightened and their words are so influential. Of all forms of earthly greatness, surely this is the most despicable."

Let us repeat, however, that Newman was not indulging irrationalism or anti-intellectualism; he was not striking out against reason but only against its limitation to a narrow circle of light, the cribbing of its fullness and richness. Newman wanted to enlarge and enliven it in the total personality. In other words, he wanted to make reason ontological as well as logical. Newman lived in the mind—there can be no question of it—but, like Pascal, Newman lived in the mind entirely. His thought was alive with love and feeling; his whole being animated his mind and his utterance. And as Bergson, Newman was attempting to renew the importance of the intuitive, the knowledge of the heart in an age in which knowledge by logic had made man skeptical. Let us remember, too, Newman's cardinalatial motto: *cor ad cor loquitur*. Newman desired that the mind be capable of the experience of spiritual reality, from which the surface movements of mental acts often estrange it. Christopher Dawson (whose *Spirit of the Oxford Movement* remains a classic of interpretation) has tried, in his *Enquiries into Religion and Culture,* to describe this essential capacity of the soul: "Underneath the surface of our ordinary consciousness, the sphere of the discursive reason, is a deeper psychological level, 'the ground of the soul' . . . this is the domain of the spiritual intuition, the 'summit' of the mind and the spiritual level which is naturally directed towards God."

Newman, somewhat in this vein, has used the term *spiritually-minded* which means "to see by faith all those good and holy beings who actually surround us, though we see them not with our bodily eyes; to see them by faith as vividly as we see the things of earth—the green country, the blue sky, and the brilliant sunshine. Hence it is that, when saintly souls are favored with heavenly visions, these visions are but the extraordinary continuations and the crown, by a divine intuition, of objects which, by the ordinary operation of grace, are ever before their minds." Briefly, Newman wished to reunite the mind and spirit, the mind and man's complete being, a unity destroyed by the rationalistic and aridly academic domination of modern thought.

The fact is that Newman's mind was fixed at the awesome point of Christ, the stitch in history, to employ Claudel's phrase, that cannot be undone. For him, as for Theodor Haecker, a spiritually-lustrous Catholic inheritor of both Kierkegaard's and Newman's thought in the twentieth century, writing in his *Journal in the Night*: 'Reflection, recollection and turning back to contemporaneity with Christ, is a requirement of *Christian thinking*. And if that capacity is lacking, a man may be a thinker of genius, where thoughts are concerned, but in the strict sense of the word he is not a *Christian* thinker. The life of Christ among men of every kind and position is so full, so complete, that in spite of the difference between life in those times and life today, every man can find a situation in which he can in all seriousness ask the question: what should I have done in that case?" Newman, whom Haecker once characterized as "saintly," would have fitted Haecker's conception of the spiritual man as different from the intellectual man, "though naturally presupposing and including him: he has a whole dimension more, he is the complete man, according to the idea of God, a perfect unity, an incomparable totality, desired by God, and, as *anima naturaliter Christiana,* longed for by man." Haecker might well see in Newman not merely the demonstrator but the communicator, with pulsing power and wondrous style, of the truth of existence. He might see in him the embodiment of the unity of spiritual life and spiritual thought, which does not signify living or thinking without the body or even against the body; it signifies living and thinking hierarchically: "Christianity aims to educate man spiritually; it is hierarchical." But man remains—grandly and warmly, in all the strength of the deep and far-flung stretch of his personality, in all the immensity of his human and eternal possibilities. And Newman the *spirituel,* the spiritually-minded, hoped and struggled valiantly to redeem the time of man and to restore the world of the fallen to the purity of its creation by God.

III

Newman's interest in the deepest realization of the personality suggests that his spirit was not just anti-rationalist but positively *humanistic*. Newman was a humanist—in the best sense. His was a Christian humanism, the humanism of the Incarnation, Maritain calls it in *True Humanism,* saying: ". . . the creature will neither be belittled nor annihilated before God, his rehabilitation will not be in contradiction to God or without God, but *in* God. There is but one way of progress for the history of the world, that is, for a Christian order, however, it may be otherwise: that the creature should be truly respected *in* his connection with God and *because* he is totally dependent on Him; humanism indeed, but a theocentric humanism, rooted in what is radical in man: integral humanism, the humanism of the Incarnation."

Thoroughly did Newman understand that to submit the human intelligence to the service of Christ the King, to use Gilson's good phrases, was not to deny the intelligence but to cherish it and complete it. Yet, as Gilson comments in *Christianity and Philosophy,* ". . . the everlasting protest of the world against Christians is that they scorn it, and that by scorning it they misunderstand what constitutes the proper value of its nature: its goodness, its beauty, its intelligibility. That explains the ceaseless reproaches directed against us, in the name of philosophy, of history, and of science. Christianity refuses to take the whole man, and, under the pretext of making him better, it mutilates him, forcing him to close his eyes to things that constitute the excellence of nature and life, to misunderstand the progress of society throughout history and to hold suspect science which progressively discloses the laws of nature and those of societies. These reproaches, repeatedly flung at us, are so familiar as to cease to interest us; nevertheless it is our duty never to cease replying to them and above all, never to lose sight ourselves of what is the reply to them. Yes, Christianity is a radical condemnation of the world, but it is at the same time an unreserved approbation of nature; for the world is not nature. It is nature shaping its course without God." These statements of Gilson, it is clear, Newman could have made too. And Newman could have subscribed to Gilson's further remarks: "What is true of nature is eminently true of the intelligence, the crown of nature. . . . There is a love of the intelligence, which consists in turning it towards visible and transient things: that belongs to the world; but there is another which consists in turning it towards the invisible and the eternal: that belongs to Christians. It is, therefore, ours; and if we prefer it to the first, it is because it does not deny us anything the first would give us, and yet it overwhelms us with everything which the other is incapable of giving us." This is a great way to indicate the mystery of the Christian man and his attitude towards life. The Christian can "love the work of God while hating sin which deforms it."

And this was the real import of Newman's approach to reality. Having had a grasp of the spirit of the liturgy, Newman also had truly the finest sense of the nature of man, as delineated by Maritain in *Education at the Crossroads*: ". . . man as an animal endowed with reason, whose supreme dignity is in the intellect, and man as a free individual in personal relation with God, whose supreme righteousness consists in voluntarily obeying the law of God; and man as a sinful and wounded creature called to divine life and the freedom of grace, whose supreme perfection consists of love." Newman had the deepest understanding of man and the problems of man. He knew that man is not to be taken "for what he is not, for something more divine and sacred." He knew that it is not the way of the world to see man or to have man as man regenerate but rather as the natural man. Newman's own definition of man has an admirable realism: "Man is composed of body and soul; he thinks and he acts; he has appetites, passions, affections, motives, designs, he has within him the lifelong struggle of duty with inclination; he has an intellect fertile and capacious; he is formed for society and society multiplies and diversifies in endless combinations his personal characteristics, moral and intellectual. All this constitutes his life. . . ." Again, Newman describes man: "Man is a being of genius, passion, intellect, conscience, power. He exercises these gifts in various ways, in great deeds, in great thoughts, in heroic acts, in hateful crimes. He founds states, he fights battles, he builds cities, he ploughs the forest, he subdues the elements, he rules his kind. He creates vast ideas, and influences many generations. He takes a thousand shapes, and undergoes a thousand fortunes. . . . He pours out his soul in fervid poetry; he sways to and fro, he soars, he dives, in his restless speculations; his lips drop eloquence; he touches the canvas, and it glows with beauty; he sweeps the strings, and they thrill with an ecstatic meaning. He looks back onto himself, and he reads his own thoughts, and notes them down; he looks out into the universe, and tells over and celebrates the elements and principles of which it is the product. Such is man. . . ."

Over this natural man, however, Newman did not despair. As a Catholic, he could not. For the wounds of nature, the mortalities of time, the Catholic believes, can be restored by the grace of Christ, the Creator and the Redeemer of nature and time. In one of the majestic and moving sermons that remain the great clue to his spirit, Newman declares: "The regenerate soul is taken into communion with saints and angels, and its life is 'hid with Christ in God.' . . . And while it obeys the instinct of the senses, it does so for God's sake, and it submits itself to things of time so far as to be brought to perfection by them, that, when the veil is withdrawn and it sees itself to be, where it has ever been, in God's Kingdom, it may be found worthy to enjoy it. It is this view of life, which removes from us all surprise and disappointment that it is so incomplete: as well might we expect any chance event which happens in the course of it to be complete, any casual conversation with a stranger, or the toil or amusement of an hour. . . . Why should we be anxious for a long life, or wealth, or credit, or comfort, who know that the next world will be everything that our hearts can wish, and that not in appearance only, but truly and everlastingly? Why should we rest in this world, when it is the token and promise of another? Why should we be content with its surface, instead of appropriating what is stored beneath it?"

For this reason Newman could not have plunged himself into darkness and despair in the face of his own or of mankind's failures. Even though he observed and experienced personally the weaknesses of man's mortality and of man's civilization, the spirit of Newman was in general not tragically tormented, not shatteringly disturbed. In this he was not quite like those men who are to be remembered with him: Kierkegaard, the Danish poet in effect and perhaps the greatest Protestant religious thinker of the nineteenth century; Brownson, the fabulous American fighter for the life of the Church, for the things that are not Caesar's; and Hopkins, the poet in fact, the seer, the spiritual son of Newman, and actually born just the year before Newman's conversion. Newman's spirit had a quiet grandeur, like the quiet ocean rolling rhythmically or like great fields moving in winds that are even. Contrastingly, the spirit of Hopkins is sometimes like the upsurging of the ocean in cliffs of tumult or like the terrible sharp pain of scythes and knives, cutting into the very grain, the vein of the soul. Newman's spirit, it seems, is more exactly akin to that of Maritain, Gilson, Guardini, Dawson, Haecker, Pieper, Marcel, or to that splendid trio of French priest-thinkers in the Church, Danielou, de Lubac, and Bouyer, the last himself a priest of the Oratory and a lifetime as well as pre-eminent student of Newman's life and spirituality. At any rate the vision and the realization are always acutely there but the suffering is less apparent than in a Hopkins or a Kierkegaard or a Bloy.

IV

Newman realized that the Christian *had to be* in the world, and face the demands of the world, even though he was not of it. This is why it is hard to understand Sean O'Faolain's statement, in tracing Newman's way, that he was tainted by "a sense of man's pitiable weakness" before God and destiny. Among other implications here is man's inadequacy to face the realities and mysteries of life. But in the sermon last cited, Newman emphasized that "the regenerate soul must submit itself to things of time so far as to be brought to perfection by them." Man possesses the strength and the grace to deal with the things of time and to improve his mortal lot. In dealing with the things of time and the problems of the world, Newman showed himself to be wonderfully sympathetic, comprehensive and various-minded; not only could he deal with theological and philosophical subjects, but he turned his mind also to historical and political and social questions, to the problems of literature in the modern world, and, notably, to the problem of the education of a man—through the humanities—in a civilization preoccupied with matter. In an important essay, done for *The Review of Politics* in April, 1945, Alvan S. Ryan reveals the development of Newman's political thought and, comparing it with that of contemporary Catholic thinkers like Maritain or Don Luigi Sturzo, concludes that Newman was "keenly alive to one of the major problems of our time," the problem of "the

Church, the State and the human person in their mutual relations" and that Newman's ideas on this difficult subject have even today "real pertinence and validity." But perhaps Newman's most striking work was his attempt to create a Catholic University, a place where his engrossment with the relationships between human and divine wisdom, his celebrated devotion to the unity of knowledge and the unity of intellect and spirit, would have an impress upon young Catholics and enable them to become true thinkers in the Church. The "failure" of the Catholic university has been duly discussed. But, as Fergal McGrath properly points out, in *Newman's University: Idea and Reality,* the record of Newman's work for the university must be seen as "the inspiring effort of a great mind to establish a perfect synthesis of the puzzling pattern of human existence, and to honour it as an ennoblement of the concept of man's destiny." And, in a certain sense, Newman's effort has received its recognition and justification not only in Ireland but in the United States. He would have been interested in and pleased by the extraordinary edifice of the higher learning built by American Catholics. Still he would have been distressed by our inveterate instinct, in the fashion of the day, to materialize rather than to spiritualize the intellect, to plunder the treasures of the soul by turning the wonderful and mysterious mind inside out in the adulation of bald facts, figures, and formulas. In times past our Catholic colleges may have tended to stress religion at the expense of intellectual development; today infected by the rationalism of the American intellectual climate, they dedicate themselves as fervently as the next to the achievement of "soullessness"—and the need to reunite the intellect and spirit is generally unrecognized. He would have been distressed by our too often programmatic, organizational, businesslike, and bureaucratic rather than personal, reverent, and organic approach to the problems of the instruction of our youth. Indeed he appositely and widely remarks: "An cademical system without the personal influence of teach-rs upon pupils, is an arctic winter; it will create an ice-bound, petrified, cast-iron University, and nothing else." Do we not recklessly multiply the rigors of an arctic winter and thus create a cast-iron rather than warmly and dynamically intellectual Catholic education? He would have been dubious about the prevailing belief that, through mere system and industriousness rather than through the free release of the spirit, we can develop first-rate excellence in our students. Discussing the formation of a Catholic literature in the English language as one of the special objects which a Catholic university ought to promote, he goes directly and sensibly to the heart of the matter: first-rate excellence in all matters is "either an accident or the outcome of a process; and in either case demands a course of years to secure. We cannot reckon on a Plato, we cannot force an Aristotle, any more than we can command a fine harvest or create a coal field."

In the variety of his humane concerns, he showed, it is said, exceptional talent in music. He wrote verse (more significant for its revelation of the mystery of Newman than anything else) and fiction. No matter how far removed from his own realm of life, he could always respect and appreciate any nobility of intellect, spirit and achievement. One of his contemporaries, James Anthony Froude, reminiscing about the high church revival, wrote of Newman justly: "Newman's mind was world-wide. . . . He had studied modern life and modern thought in all its forms. . . . He was interested in everything. . . . Nothing was too large for him, nothing too trivial, if it threw light upon the central question, what man really was and what was his destiny. . . . He seemed always to be better informed on common topics of conversation than anyone else who was present. He was never condescending with us, never didactic or authoritative; but what he said carried conviction along with it. When we were wrong he knew why we were wrong and excused our mistakes to ourselves,

while he set us right. Perhaps his supreme merit as a talk
er was that he never tried to be witty or say strikin
things. Ironical he could be, but not ill-natured. Not
malicious anecdote was ever heard from him. Prosy h
could not be. He was lightness itself—the lightness c
elastic strength . . . we had never seen such another ma
. . . he was careless about his personal prospects. He ha
no ambitions to make a career, or to rise to rank an
power. Still less had pleasure any seductions for him. H
natural temperament was bright and light; his senses, eve
the commonest, were exceptionally delicate. I was tol
that, though he rarely drank wine, he was trusted to choos
the vintages for the college cellar" (quoted from W. F
Stockley in his *Newman, Education and Ireland*). Thi
then, is a portrait of a highly civilized as well as a gen
inely distinguished person, a man of grace and sensibilit
and control.

V

Because he was what he was, Newman could not abid
the Philistine, the creature who is, in Arnold's terms, vu
gar in beauty and taste, coarse in morals and feeling, an
dull in mind and spirit. He could not comprehend th
bourgeois mind, the enemy of light and the children c
light. His spirit was hierarchical and aristocratic in th
finest way, that is, he was anti-mediocre, hostile not t
the people but to mob-judgments and mob-standards, hos
tile to the complacency, the pharisaism, the traps of rou
tine and the spirit of dead-leveling, the lack of order an
distinction in modern civilization. He understood, lik
Kierkegaard, Bloy, Péguy and Bernanos, how essentiall
unheroic, undistinguished the spirit of modern man i
how fearful of taking real risks, how desirous of comfor
able physical security, how indifferent to the true com
fort of the soul—in his own word, how *tepid*. Newma
says of small souls: "They who are ever taking aim, mak

o hits; they who never venture, never gain; to be ever afe is to be ever feeble." And he advises against bourgeois prudence: "Calculation never made a hero"; "Every reat change is effected by the few, not the many; by the esolute, undaunted, zealous few," that is to say, by those who are not mediocre, not tepid, who are willing, right in the spirit of Christ, to give themselves for others.

But the warm, vibrant spirit of Christ and His Church does not prevail in the cold, mechanic reaches of modern civilization. Instead the spirit of The Public flourishes and overwhelms, a spirit brilliantly described by Kierkegaard, in *The Present Age,* as a gruesome abstraction: "the public is neither a nation, nor a generation, nor a community, nor a society, nor these particular men, for all these are only what they are through the concrete. No single person who belongs to the public makes a real commitment . . . a public is a kind of gigantic something, an abstract and deserted void which is everything and nothing . . . a public is something which everyone can claim . . . the most dangerous of all powers and the most insignificant: one can speak to a whole nation in the name of the public and still the public will be less than a single real man, however unimportant." And Kierkegaard adds: "More and more individuals, owing to their bloodless indolence, will aspire to be nothing at all—in order to become the public." Similarly but more moderately, Newman reflects upon the public in terms of public opinion, which he says he would not be so irrational as to despise. Still, he expresses the feeling that too often it is nothing else than what the whole world opines, and no one in particular. Your neighbour assures you that everyone is of one way of thinking; that there is but one opinion on the subject; and while he claims not to be answerable for it, he does not hesitate to propound and spread it. In such cases, everyone is appealing to everyone else; and the constituent members of a community one by one think it their duty to defer and succumb to the voice of that same community as whole."

103

In an era, then, that has succumbed to "the public," in an age of massification, what happens to the Christian and the Christian nation? Kierkegaard bluntly replies in his *Attack upon "Christendom"*: "We are what is called a 'Christian' nation—but in such a sense that not a single one of us is in the character of the Christianity of the New Testament. . . . The illusion of a Christian nation is due doubtless to the power which number exercise over the imagination." Likewise, Newman summarizes the real life-situation of most men known as Christians: they "would go on almost as they do, neither much better nor much worse, if they believed Christianity to be a fable. When young, they indulge their lusts, or at least pursue the world's vanities; as time goes on, they get into a fair way of business, or other mode of making money; then they marry and settle; and their interest coinciding with their duty, they seem to be, and think themselves respectable and religious men; they grow attached to things as they are; they begin to have a zeal against vice and error; and they follow after peace with all men. Such conduct indeed, as far as it goes, is right and praiseworthy. Only I say, it has not necessarily anything to do with religion at all. . . ." These men called Christians "venture nothing, they risk, they sacrifice, they abandon nothing on the faith of Christ's words." The Christian man, the Christian mind is "religious morning, noon, and night; his religion is a certain character, a mould in which his thoughts words and actions are cast, all forming parts of one and the same whole. He sees God in all things; every course of action he directs towards those spiritual objects which God has revealed to him; every occurrence of the day every event, every person met with, all news which he hears, he measures by the standard of God's will. And person who does this may be said almost literally to pray without ceasing." The Christian mind is one "ever marveling, and irreligious men laugh and scoff at it because it marvels." Out of the wonder of the Christian mysteries he faithful and prayerful mind will be raised, refined, made reverent and expectant.

Yet Newman discerned the rarity of such men and minds in the midst of progressive modern civilization. It cannot be said that Newman did not understand the need for civilization. He realized and said that civilization is the state to which man's nature points and tends; it represents the "use, improvement, and combination of those faculties which are his characteristic; and, viewed in its idea, it is the perfection, the happiness of our mortal state." But the civilization of his experience, with its neglect and omission of the Christ-form in human thought and action, with its frustration and misuse of the graces and purposes of Christ's Church in history, simply was not contributing to the perfection and happiness of our mortal state. It was contributing only to the death of spirituality. So there rises from the very soul of Newman the absolute anguish—not normal for him—caught into the overpowering pressure of this unforgettable utterance, a cosmic cry of pain, where he wonders what will ever now, in civilization itself, help to arrest the onward course of wilful and perverse human nature: "Starting then with the being of a God (which, as I have said, is as certain to me as the certainty of my own existence, though when I try to put the grounds of that certainty into logical shape I find a difficulty in doing so in mood and figure to my satisfaction,) I look out of myself into the world of men, and there I see a sight which fills me with unspeakable distress. The world seems simply to give the lie to that great truth, of which my whole being is so full; and the effect upon me is, in consequence, as a matter of necessity, as confusing as if it denied that I am in existence myself. If I looked into a mirror and did not see my face, I should have the sort of feeling which actually comes upon me, when I look into this living busy world, and see no reflection of its creator. This is to me one of those great difficulties of this absolute primary truth, to which I referred just now. Were it not for this voice, speaking so clearly in my conscience and my heart, I should be an atheist, or a pantheist, or a polytheist when I looked into the world. I am speaking for myself only; and I am far from denying the real force of the arguments in proof of a God, drawn from the general facts of human society and the course of history, but these do not warm me nor enlighten me, they do not take away the winter of my desolation, or make the buds unfold and the leaves grow within me, and my moral being rejoice. The sight of the world is nothing else than the prophet's scroll, full of 'lamentations and mourning and woe'."

The very complication and prolongation of the texture and structure of this remarkable sentence carry the intense and complex passion of the suffering and heartful mind of Newman: "To consider the world, its length and breadth, its various history, the many races of men, their starts, their fortunes, their mutual alienation, their conflicts; and then their ways, habits, governments, forms of worship, their enterprises, their aimless courses, their random achievements and acquirements, the impotent conclusion of long-standing facts, the token so faint and broken of a superintending design, the blind evolution of what turn out to be great powers or truths, the progress of things, as if from unreasoning elements, not towards final causes, the greatness and littleness of man, his far-reaching aims, his short duration, the curtain hung over his futurity, the disappointments of life, the defeat of good, the success of evil, physical pain, mental anguish, the prevalence and intensity of sin, the pervading idolatries, the corruptions, the dreary hopeless irreligion, that condition of the whole race so fearfully yet exactly described in the Apostle's words, 'having no hope and without God in the world,'—all this is a vision to dizzy and appall; and inflicts upon the mind the sense of a profound mystery, which is absolutely beyond human solution."

All this does not mean that Newman rejected nature or civilization. It means only that he could not endure a world going its own defiantly irreligious and irreverent way. It means that Newman, the Catholic, the sensitive realist and "imperial intellect" could not help being dizzied and appalled by the debased and debasing features of modern civilization. As the magistral and spiritually-minded thinker in the Church, completing himself within the spirit of the liturgy, Newman had ever to be against progressing with the untoward spirit of the age. Unfortunately, too many of us as members and thinkers of the Church in America, even while we take the name of Newman, move against his spirit. We are daily capable of demonstration, systematization, "objectivity," analysis, examination and self-examination, not to mention administration. But we are not capable of Newman's power of "communication," of his "realization," of transforming by our touch all that comes before us in human existence. We do not live in the reality, the self-subjection of the liturgy. We live by formulas and slogans and calculations. We weave arguments and wield propositions but we lack spiritual vision. We are not people of heart, people of love. We are, as any occasion requires, narrow and partisan and prejudiced. We are unwilling honestly and dynamically out of our own resources and values provided by the Church to deal with the problems of time, in politics or education or literature or science, because we tend to regard our light and our truth as inferior, as inadequate; we do not respect it enough; so we are afraid that it will fail. We are not proud of it and we will not try it. We are "reflective" —in the Kierkegaardian meaning: we mirror, echo, reflect our environment instead of returning to Christ His image. We merely imitate the ways of the world and provide little light or "eternal form" to it. We are not really too sure about what man is or man's society. In our conception of order and discipline, we are calvinists: we do not really regard man as regenerate, as open to grace though wounded. We rush into darkness and despair when failure befalls our enterprises. Or, mediocre in spirit, we do not attempt anything at all lest our set ways be altered seriously. We make progress only in routine or in things that are external. We like our realities to be huge, statistical and public. We seem incapable of true inwardness as well as openness, of "marveling." We work hard to organize and mechanize the spirit, to destroy its standards and values and hierarchies. We level the spirit and bury it and, in unmarked graves, we bury ourselves with it. Our poor spirit is clearly not the rich and full spirit of Newman. It is instead the spirit of the age. But we are pharisaical. We breathe the name of Newman and incinerate his being. On the earth that is moving onwards we live by our wits—and on the verge of nothing. Intellectually and spiritually—and humanly—we perish. And we perish in pathetic poverty.

NOTE

1 The pattern of Newman's spirit is drawn through his words —most of them long familiar to his American readers— chiefly from the following volumes, listed in order of appearance in the text: *Lectures on Justification, Parochial and Plain Sermons, IV, V, Discussions and Arguments, Loss and Gain, Oxford University Sermons, An Essay in Aid of a Grammar of Assent, Essays Critical and Historical, Sermons on Subjects of the Day, Meditations and Devotions, The Idea of a University, Historical Sketches III,* and *Apologia Pro Vita Sua.*

BIBLIOGRAPHY

Blehl, Vincent F., and Francis X. Connolly, eds. *Newman's Apologia*: *A Classic Reconsidered*. New York, 1964.

Bouyer, Louis. *Newman*: *His Life and Spirituality*. London, 1958.

Harrold, Charles F. *John Henry Newman*: *An Expository and Critical Study of His Mind, Thought and Art*. New York, 1945.

McGrath, Fergal. *The Consecration of Learning*. New York, 1962.

Newman, John Henry. *Works*. 40 vols. London, 1874-1921.

Ward, Wilfrid. *The Life of John Henry Cardinal Newman*. London, 1912.

CONTRIBUTORS

HAROLD M. PETITPAS is an Associate Professor of English at Seton Hall University.

JOHN PICK is a Professor of English at Marquette University and the Editor of *Renascence*. In 1952 he published *Gerard Manley Hopkins* and *A Hopkins Reader* in 1953.

FRANK O'MALLEY is a Professor of English at Notre Dame and Associate Editor of *The Review of Politics*.

NORTHROP FRYE is a professor of English at Victoria College, the University of Toronto. His *Anatomy of Criticism* is a landmark in literary criticism. He is also the author of *Fearful Symmetry*.

FATHER WALTER ONG, S.J. is a Professor of English at St. Louis University. His books include: *American Catholic Crossroads, In the Human Grain,* and *The Presence of the Word.*

JOSEPH HOUPPERT is an Assistant Professor of English at the University of Maryland. He has published in *Renaissance News* and is the editor of the forthcoming edition of Thomas Lodge's *The Wounds of Civil War* (Regents Renaissance Drama Series).